PunditMom's
Mothers
of Intention

HOW WOMEN & SOCIAL MEDIA ARE
REVOLUTIONIZING POLITICS IN AMERICA

JOANNE BAMBERGER

{ Having An Opinion Never Goes Out Of Style }

bright sky press
HOUSTON, TEXAS

bright sky press
HOUSTON, TEXAS

2365 Rice Boulevard, Suite 202,
Houston, Texas 77005

10 9 8 7 6 5 4 3 2 1

Library of Congress Cataloging-in-Publication Data on file with publisher.

Editorial Director, Lucy H. Chambers; Editors, Cristina Adams and Kristen Latta
Creative Director, Ellen P. Cregan; Designer, Marla Garcia.
Printed in Canada

TABLE of CONTENTS

For my husband David and my
daughter Rachel, my two biggest
supporters in the entire world,
whose patience, love and understanding
made this book possible

PREFACE

Joanne Bamberger has a habit of grabbing the spotlight and immediately turning it toward other women.

I speak from experience.

In the fall of 2007, Joanne invited me to give a talk to the American News Women's Club in Washington D.C.

"You will *love* these women," she said.

How could I say no?

Four years later, I can still picture Joanne on that evening—darting like a firefly from one woman to another, gently guiding them over to me with a big smile on her face.

Every time, she would introduce the woman, then wrap her arm around her and say, "Now, tell Connie all about you." How those stories tumbled out, and each time Joanne leaned in next to me, wide-eyed and nodding as if she were hearing all of them for the very first time.

Mothers of Intention is the kind of book

that can only come from a writer certain enough of her own narrative that she'd rather invest in other women's stories. In the truest sense, Joanne—whom many of us know first and foremost as PunditMom—has outdone herself by raising the voices of mothers like her, who blog. She could have taken an easier route to her first book. A feminist to her core, she could have joined the growing number of authors who fill hundreds of pages with examples of the mainstream media depicting the opinions of women, particularly mothers, as whispers on the sidelines. Slap on a clever cover illustration –a woman lost in the shadows, maybe?—and then hit the circuit lecturing male pundits about their lack of a clue.

But that would be a message of our collective helplessness, and that is not Joanne's style. Instead of leading with our injuries, she has collected 216 pages of irrefutable proof that America is full of smart and engaged women whose political activism has been unleashed by the joys and challenges of motherhood. And they write, too. Lord, how they write.

"Yes, we're mothers," Joanne writes. "Yes, we're bloggers. But when the media describe what women do, they often invoke diminutive vocabulary as a way to suggest that there's no need to take us seriously."

Joanne's book puts that little myth to rest for good.

You are about to meet some remarkable women in this book. Opinionated mothers, every last one of them. You won't agree with all of them, but if you're a woman you already know that. We're a diverse gender, and always have been—even when no one was listening.

I confess to occasional bouts of envy as I read the opinions of these young mothers, and Joanne's graceful essays that tie them together. How I wish this online community of mothers had existed when I was a young mom, full of opinions but afraid no one was listening. On the other hand, Joanne's book reminds me of my journalist's debt to the mothers who went before me. Most of my early breaks in essay writing came from editors who were also mothers. For years I wanted to be a columnist, but every male editor said no. In 2002, two women—both mothers of young children—finally excavated the way. Looking back, I can see those two women were very much like Joanne Bamberger: They got promoted, and quickly yanked me onstage.

Joanne's own stage keeps getting bigger, but will never be lonely. If I were a cartoonist, I would draw her as a cheerful woman in funky glasses and multiple arms waving to women in the audience and shouting, "You! Yes, you! Come stand next to me. And you! C'mon. Bring those three women behind you, too. Plenty of room."

What do you call a mother like that?

"If we're going to resort to labels," Joanne writes, "I like 'cause mom' better than the few the media seem to be stuck with, like 'soccer moms,' 'security moms,' 'Wal-Mart moms,' or 'maxed-out' moms."

Agreed.

But dear Joanne, after reading your book, another label comes to mind.

Call me a 'grateful mom'.

Connie Schultz
January 2011

INTRODUCTION

Mothers are political. If you don't think that's true, think again.

When children become part of our lives, we're committed to making the world a better place for them as they grow up. But we live in a culture where mothers often are undervalued and overlooked, so many people assume that once we have children, thoughts of anything unrelated to the care and feeding of kids flees our minds, our political thoughts and goals dismissed. As a result, it's often difficult for women with children to be considered serious political actors. In the age of the "mommy wars," mothers' opinions frequently are viewed as somehow less worthy of consideration than those of so-called experts, or even of women who don't self-identify as mothers.

The good news for mothers is this—the advent of the online world of the blogosphere and social media is changing that forever.

A commonly shared story among women is that when we become mothers, people stop listening to us at cocktail parties. Even if we were the neighborhood's most interesting girls in our pre-motherhood days with a life full of personal and professional accomplishments who made the best small talk in town, many of us discovered that when we brought up the topic of our children, we'd get tuned out by those who assumed we'd chat about nothing but potty training, pre-school and playgrounds. Often people make the assumption that with the birth or adoption of a child, interesting things get sucked from women's brains, replaced only by the mundane. I didn't believe it until I lived it and clearly remember my thought bubble the first time it happened—*"You really think I'm less smart or interesting now that I'm a mother?!"*

For twenty-plus years as a working professional, I always had an answer to the opening party question, *"What do you do?"* People seemed interested—at least after a glass of wine or an apple martini—in what I, as a journalist, lawyer, or deputy director of a federal agency public affairs office, had to say. How in the world could that change overnight just because I became a mother? I still had my experience and my education. I saw the headlines of the newspapers and caught enough cable news to discuss more than diapers and teething. And I was, on most days, still able to put together a coherent sentence.

But I learned that it didn't matter.

The same types of people who had been happy enough to chat with me about politics, current events or any of a million other topics, were no longer interested in hearing what I had to say. The first time I replied to the 'what-do-you-do' question with information about having returned from China after adopting our wonderful daughter and said that I was taking time off from the workplace, eyes glazed over in that semi-polite 'I-need-another-cocktail' way before I could even mention the nice title of my previous job. Even as I tried to regroup in those situations with statements like, *"When I was practicing law ....,"* or *"Did you see the headline about ...."* or even *"Did I tell you about the time I met Henry Kissinger ....,"* it was clear that what I had to say no longer mattered. The "M" word had caused me to become irrelevant.

Those experiences reminded me of the popular *Far Side* cartoon that featured two panels—"What we say to dogs" *(Okay, Ginger, I've had it! You stay out of the garbage!)* and "What they hear" *(Blah, blah Ginger, blah, blah, blah, blah).* After stating my name, anything I said in those social settings became mere background noise. *Blah, blah, blah.*

I also came to the realization that cocktail parties aren't the only venue where mothers' voices and opinions are dismissed. The worlds of work, pop culture, movies, and politics do their fair share to keep us boxed into an outdated vision of American motherhood, one that portrays us as forsaking our education and intellect at the altar of opt-out motherhood.

Many mothers share the experience of not being taken seriously in the workplace. Their professional status is often undercut as they find themselves left out of important work meetings because it's assumed, incorrectly and stereotypically, that they can't be counted on because priorities have shifted to their children to the exclusion of everything else. This phenomenon has become so prevalent that academics have dubbed it one aspect of the "motherhood penalty."[1]

Popular culture feeds that perception as it continues to reinforce an outdated version of American motherhood. Television commercials and magazine ads show us wiping spills and wiping noses. Our writing gets pushed aside with the condescending descriptions "mommy blogs" and "chick lit." The notion that mothers are political influencers is openly scoffed at on cable news shows, even though new research confirms that.[2] Twenty-first century mothers as a group are portrayed in the media as a monolith—or should I say "momolith"—more concerned with clipping coupons and baby carriers as fashion statement[3] than with current events, the state of the world or what we can do to make a difference for our children's future. There are few pop culture portrayals of mothers, even those who work full-time outside the home, who are more than Carol Brady throw-backs—giddy over a new Swiffer[4], happy as the kiddie chauffeur, and eagerly taking the "opt-out" from professional life to become a stay-at-home mom.[5]

Hollywood plays its role in further advancing these stereotypes. Screenwriter Nora Ephron has said it's because men just can't figure out women. They are stuck in their assumptions that the only movies worth making are ones aimed at the audience they know—boys and men.[6] They just don't know how to market to women, especially women over 30. Or perhaps they don't care to.

Similar marginalization of women's views and voices is also present in the world of political commentary.[7] Evidence of that is reflected in a *Vanity Fair* article about the rise of the political website and newspaper, *Politico.*[8] *Politico* was created in 2007 to be a fresh voice and new way of thinking in the world of political reporting and analysis, yet it was represented in a 2010 article in that magazine with a photo of four smiling men, strolling through the office's hallway, looking very content as the crew running the enterprise.

When there is an interest in the voices of women and mothers in the political world, it has largely been when politicians or special interest groups see a particular version of motherhood as a way to frame their own perspectives, rather than engaging in actual discussion or exploring the unique view that mothers bring to the spectrum of political issues. Politicians wonder—*What do the 'soccer moms' want?*[9] *What are those 'security moms' focused on?* In the 2010 midterm elections, we were talked about in terms of being 'Wal-Mart moms'[10] and 'weary working women.'[11] Elected officials, pollsters, and campaign representatives continue to present neatly packaged talking points aimed at the latest stereotype of motherhood and serve them up as their way to win our votes (and our dollars).[12] But our male-heavy political and media worlds remain, for the most part, distinctly indifferent to actually hearing what women in general, and mothers in particular, have to say about the world they want and how they want to shape it.

The funny thing is this: there's nothing really new about women trying to make their voices heard in the world of politics and social issues. Mothers look at life through the future-oriented lens of children. In her books *Founding Mothers* and *Ladies of Liberty, ABC News* journalist Cokie Roberts describes how the lives of the "founding mothers" touched the political world in a new America. Suffragists fought for the Nineteenth Amendment to the Constitution for themselves, as well as for their daughters. And in her book *The Feminine Mystique,* Betty Friedan clearly envisioned a world where women were viewed as more than the sum of their parenting experiences and marriage status.

Women have long strived to be heard on the political front, but the measure of success in traditional media outlets has been incredibly small. On average, only about 17 percent of op-ed commentaries in major newspapers are written by women. The numbers are only slightly better when it comes to women thought leaders on "talking head" news shows.[13] In many areas, including elective office, women's voices aren't represented in numbers anywhere close to those of men.[14]

The few traditional media opportunities for women seem to be dwindling. The winners of the 2009 and 2010 "Next Great Pundit Contests" at the *Washington Post* were men; the latest writer to be promoted to the main opinion page of the *Washington Post* was another man, Dana Milbank. And with the retirements of columnists Ellen Goodman and Anna Quindlen, the departure of Judith Warner from her weekly column at the online version of the *New York Times,* and the demise of *Politics Daily* and its *Woman Up* column, there aren't many recognized mothers' voices in political opinion writing today.

One explanation for this phenomenon is that women, especially mothers, are often seen as a special-interest group with stereotypical niche concerns that don't play well with a general audience—that's how we keep getting pigeonholed as being more interested in soccer, security, and Wal-Mart discounts than in full participation in the political world. If that's the accepted portrait that's been painted of women, why *would* anyone pay attention?

Lisa Witter and Lisa Chen, authors of *The She Spot: Why Women are the Market for Changing the World—And How to Reach Them,*[15] know why influencers should be paying attention—women are not a niche audience, they are *the* audience. There are more of us. We control the vast majority of dollars spent in our homes (about 80 percent), *and* we are the key to social change. But if women are continually turned away from, or not invited into, the male-dominated club of political commentary, where can they turn to make a bigger splash with their voices and opinions? The answer is easier than it was just a few years ago: the online world of social media.

Myriad numbers of women not only are carving out their own spaces on blogs and social networks, such as Facebook and Twitter, but they are also the majority users of those venues.[16] The relatively new tools in the online world are built on networking and developing communities, skills that women cultivate every day in their personal and professional lives. So, figuratively, the online world was made for women. Now, no matter what others choose to call us or whether they call on us as political analysts or commentators on current events, women can and are becoming politically empowered as a direct result of the new media opportunities that have far fewer barriers to entry than in traditional media.

Even with increasing types of platforms in the brave new world of social media, like blogs, micro-blogs, and fan pages, women who self-identify as mothers and who embrace political views informed by their parental status still face the challenge of being heard in a sea of over 150 million blogs. In the world of pundits and politicos, unless one is affiliated with an established group political site like *Huffington Post, Daily Kos, Real Clear Politics, Talking Points Memo* or *Red State,* it's difficult to break through the din to becoming political influencers. Fortunately, more and more women, especially mothers, have started using their existing online spaces—the so-called "mom blogs"—and the confidence they've gained through the influence they have earned in those spaces, to flex their political muscles. Increasing numbers of mothers online are embracing the newfound courage that's developed from writing about their lives and families to speak out for causes, social issues, and candidates they believe in, moving from writing about their beliefs at personal blogs to creating their own online political communities and joining established networks that already reach millions of readers.

Political leaders and officials are seeking us out—we're being invited to the White House and we're being asked to participate in meetings and conference calls with national leaders like consumer finance watchdog Elizabeth Warren, presidential advisors David Axelrod and Valerie Jarrett, and many others. Mothers who have found their activist voices online are being asked to speak at political conferences and, occasionally, have been added to the ranks of cable news analysts to talk about topics ranging from Sarah Palin's vice-presidential candidacy to Supreme Court nominees[17] to election night coverage.

This growing phenomenon of women as influencers online is more than supported by the numbers. According to a 2009 study by *BlogHer* and Compass Partners, 79 million women a week are online,[18] and that number only continues to grow. Forty-two million of those are considered to be "active" users, meaning they go online at least once a week. More than 31 million women a week use some sort of social networking tool, such as Facebook or MySpace, and 23 million women a week write on blogs. As for the world of politics, it's notable that almost 60 percent of those polled for the *BlogHer* study relied on blogs for political information rather than more traditional news sources.

Women are on the cutting edge of social media[19] and the odds are that the majority of those women are mothers. From Twitter to Facebook to MySpace to blogs,[20] women are leading the way in online presence and influence.[21] It's easy to see that connecting online can lead to connecting politically in the real world—women are finding common communities in the Internet world to create a true motherhood political movement that was hard to identify just a few years ago.[22]

When I started writing about the intersection of motherhood and politics at *PunditMom* blog in 2006, there were few mothers' voices in the online political arena. So I was on the lookout for others, even if they didn't agree with me politically, because I believed this was an opportunity to start an important conversation with other women, particularly mothers.

The number of mothers who were online writing about politics exploded in the run-up to the 2008 presidential election. I believe that happened, not only because of the historic nature of that presidential race with Barack Obama as the first viable African-American presidential candidate and Hillary Clinton as the first viable woman presidential candidate, but also because of the increased ability of women to express themselves online with no barriers or limits, unlike in previous elections.[23] While it is extremely difficult for even established writers to get political commentary placed in publications that policymakers read and rely on to help shape their views, like the *New York Times,* or to snag a spot on a popular news show, it's easy to find online venues in which to have political conversations, express opinions and get involved with changing the political landscape. Networking sites and blogs are the tools that allow like-minded mothers to find each other, organize, campaign, and participate more easily than ever before. Social media has become an accepted and respected entrée for getting a seat at the political table, and increasing numbers of women are pulling up their chairs to have political conversations with the big boys.[24] And there's no going back.

Websites, blogs, and other organizations, such as *MomsRising, MOMocrats, Mothers Acting Up, Help a Mother Out, Mother Talkers, She Acts, Smart Girl Politics, The Kitchen Cabinet, As a Mom, Moms4SarahPalin, The Mom Slant, MOTHERS (Mothers Ought to Have Equal Rights), Political Mommentary, The Mother PAC, TheMotherhood* and *Candid Conservative,* are merely a few of the places online where mothers are organizing around shared beliefs and values. But there's also plenty of political writing at personal and community blogs. It's just a little harder to find if you don't know it's out there. That's how this book, *Mothers of Intention,* was born.

The inspiration to write this book happened as I discovered the growing numbers of mothers who were taking their writing and on-line involvement to a new level. They may have started out as what have come to be known, sometimes condescendingly, as "mom blogs." But woven into the stories of their daily lives were the living examples of political motherhood—teaching children about homelessness, unex-pectedly finding themselves without health insurance, or being inspired to speak out for or against political candidates. I also realized that it was past time to dispel the twenty-first-century pop-culture myth that moth-ers are turning their backs on the intellectual and remind the traditional media that labeling modern motherhood as a simpler, June Cleaver ver-sion of itself is just plain wrong.

The essays gathered for *Mothers of Intention,* as well as the voices of the women who were interviewed for this book, are just a slice of the growing motherhood political pie.[25] The brave new world of female online involvement started long before Sarah Palin invoked the image of her "mama grizzlies"[26]; the essays included here are proof of that. "Mothers of intention" have strong, powerful, thoughtful, and humor-ous voices. They have plenty to say about the world today with the goal of leaving it in better shape for their children. But that doesn't mean all their political thoughts deal with what have traditionally been called "mom" issues. The topics they write about range from security issues, the wars in Iraq and Afghanistan, the economy, sexism, political double standards, and so much more.

Mothers of intention are diverse in geography, ethnicity, age, and political persuasion. They are passionate, thoughtful, and energized and have plenty to say when it comes to the entire spectrum of the issues we face. The numbers of these mothers speaking out about causes and can-didates grow every day. And by the time we reach the next presidential election, you'll have heard more from them—because these politically energized mothers aren't going away. The narrative of how mothers have used the online world to make their voices heard is a powerful one that should be told to remind pundits, politicians, and policy-makers that women with children are a force to be reckoned with.

We're mothers with blogs and we're not afraid to use them.

CHAPTER ONE

Becoming
Political
Mothers

" **I** was never so interested and engaged in politics until it became personal when I was first pregnant. All of a sudden I examined the world with new eyes and knew for sure that I needed to do something to make it better for my child."

The above e-mail arrived in my inbox one day in 2009 asking me to help get the word out about an organization fighting against the use of chemicals in children's toys, clothes, and bedding. While I hadn't heard of the particular group before receiving their e-mail, the sentiment was a common one I'd heard from countless mothers, especially after the birth of online communities and social networking.

On our journeys to becoming political mothers, we all have different timelines. For some of us, the road to political motherhood was paved in our teen years before marriage or children were on our radar; others came to the political world after becoming parents, realizing that they want and need to know they've done their part to create the world they want for their kids. Our epiphanies hit us in various ways, but the stories of how mothers discover their political identities are compelling evidence that all kinds of women are embracing the activist side of motherhood. Many women I've asked agree that motherhood made them more political because of their investment in their children's futures—in essence, becoming parents upped the ante for them in the human sweepstakes.

Examples of political motherhood are everywhere—from the White House to the movie house to the houses in our neighborhoods—but they have taken on significant cultural importance since the presidential election of 2008. This is thanks largely to increasingly utilized social media tools and high-profile mothers like First Lady Michelle Obama and former Alaska Governor Sarah Palin, who have been catalysts in how political mothers are viewed.[27]

When Sarah Palin was chosen as John McCain's running mate in 2008, the mother of five proudly embraced her status as a political mom with the now infamous question in her nomination acceptance speech, *"What's the difference between a pit bull and a hockey mom?"* (Lipstick, remember?) As she traveled the country campaigning, Palin didn't skirt the issue of her motherhood status; she wrapped herself in it and incorporated her self-proclaimed hockey mom identity as an integral part of her political persona. In her view, mothers of small children are not only capable of running for office, but the very experience of having and raising those children is an important factor in informing political views and a training ground for elective office.

The media had a difficult time dissecting candidate Palin, who didn't fit the usual stereotype of mothers or politicians. Even though she was still the governor of Alaska at that time, little was known about her in the lower forty-eight aside from a profile in *Vogue* magazine.[28] Did Palin embody an unflinching boldness by putting her motherhood status front and center into national politics, or was it mere stagecraft? Whichever version one chose to believe, the media coverage of Palin had one faulty underlying premise—that she was a new version of political motherhood in America. As people tried to get their heads around the idea of a mother of several children, including a newborn with Down Syndrome, who would be audacious enough to take on the vice presidency, news stories exploded in the media, with headlines like, *"Can Politics and Motherhood Mix?"*[29], *"Are Motherhood Politics a Good Idea?,"*[30] and *Fusing Politics and Motherhood in a New Way.*[31]

Political analysts and voters alike were shocked as Palin unexpectedly wore her motherhood on her sleeve. Until she entered the 2008 presidential race, one's motherhood status was considered mostly off-limits in politics—something either to be avoided for fear of being perceived as a weak candidate[32] or to be invoked only as a softening factor, as political consultants tried to do late in the campaign with then-Democratic presidential candidate Hillary Clinton. While the idea of motherhood identity politics was generally eschewed before 2008, it became the fashionable, new trend for the media with the arrival of Palin on the national scene.

That fascination coverage wasn't limited to Palin. First Lady Michelle Obama's political persona was initially on the more traditional "mom-in-chief" side during her husband's presidential campaign, as she focused on issues of struggling American families. However, when she took to the campaign trail during the 2010 midterm elections it was with the message about her political views and and how they were definitely filtered through "the prism of motherhood:"[33]

"[M]ore than anything else, I come at this as a mom. When I think about the issues facing our nation, I think about what it means for my girls, and I think about what it means for the world we're leaving for them and for all our children. As I travel around this country, and look into the eyes of every single child I meet, I see what's at stake."[34]

Sometime between the GOP presidential loss in 2008 and the midterm elections two years later, Palin threw a similar curveball at our cultural perceptions of politically conservative mothers, carrying motherhood identity politics even further. In 2010, she created the model of the conservative "mama grizzlies,"[35] using rugged Alaskan imagery of a mother grizzly bear rising up on its hind legs to protect its cubs as an analogy for the political strength of conservative mothers.[36] While Palin's vision of political motherhood was playing well with GOP moms plenty of women didn't see eye-to-eye with her increasingly aggressive view of the political motherhood landscape.[37] While clever, Palin's marketing effort with the mama grizzly campaign was faulty in suggesting that her so-called mom awakening was a new phenomenon and that it was exclusive to the conservative movement.

Nothing could have been further from the truth.

The general theme—that mothers see the world differently, and more politically, when they view it through the lens of what is at stake for their children's future—is a actually a common one.[38] Plenty of women from all over the country— and all over the blogosphere—of different ages and backgrounds have been a part of this under-the-media-radar wave long before Sarah Palin and Michelle Obama, and it continues to grow by leaps and bounds thanks to the brave new world of social media.

One of my favorite stories about motherhood as a political motivator belongs to U.S. Senator Amy Klobuchar from Minnesota. When Klobuchar gave birth to her daughter in 1995, she was forced to leave the hospital after 24 hours, even though her daughter Abigail was born with medical issues that required her to stay in the hospital after Klobuchar was discharged. As a result, Klobuchar mobilized a group of her pregnant friends and made sure they were present at the Minnesota hearings on requiring insurers to allow new mothers to stay in the hospital for up to forty-eight hours. As she tells the story, the chances of that legislation getting passed didn't look good, but the pregnant women outnumbered the lobbyists present, and they were able to convince the lawmakers to pass the bill immediately:

"What I most remember from the legislative battle is when we showed up at the conference committee, there were a number of lobbyists there for the insurance industry who wanted to delay it. And they couldn't come out and say it, but they were trying to delay the implementation of the bill by a year or two. And so I decided I would bring enough pregnant friends of mine so they would outnumber the insurance lobbyists [two to one] and when the [legislators] on the conference committee asked, 'Well, when should this bill take effect?' All the pregnant women raised their hands and said, 'Now!' and that's what happened."[39]

A wise lesson learned—you just don't get in the way of angry, activist pregnant women!

Klobuchar isn't the only senator whose political inspiration has come from mothers. U.S. Senator Kirsten Gillibrand of New York, a mother of two young sons, decided to run for Congress in 2006 in part because of the women in her family, including her grandmother, who organized and convinced many mothers of her generation to raise their political voices.

Gillibrand recounts, "From a young age, I watched and learned from my grandmother, Polly Noonan, who was secretary for the state legislature in Albany, New York. She decided that to have a voice on issues she cared about, she would have to join with other women to be heard. So she started organizing women to be a part of the democratic process. My grandmother and her friends focused on the grassroots—they stuffed envelopes, knocked on doors, and ran the fundamental nuts and bolts of campaigns. They ultimately became a major force in Albany."[40]

The lessons learned from her family have served Gillibrand well. The granddaughter of the one-time president of the Albany County Women's Democratic Club handily won election in 2010 to the Senate seat to which she was appointed in 2009 when Hillary Clinton stepped down to become secretary of state in President Obama's administration. Gillibrand may be a long way from the era of women being limited to support roles in politics, but her grandmother's actions were no less inspiring to her.

Motherhood can also turbo-charge a woman's political involvement, even if she's already been steeped in activism for years. Kim Gandy—former president of the National Organization for Women and the current vice president and general counsel of the Feminist Majority Foundation—was a leading women's activist for two decades before she became a mother. In both her personal and professional life, she was committed to advancing the cause of women's rights in America long before anyone called her "mommy." There was a time when she couldn't imagine that her political passion could ever be any greater. She was wrong.

"When I became a mother, my commitment to women's issues exploded in a way I hadn't realized was possible. I thought I was as committed as I could be, having been involved in activism for women's rights for 20 years. But when I had my first daughter, I knew I didn't want to spend the next 20 years of her life working for [the equality] that ought to be her birthright."[41] While it wasn't humanly possible for Gandy to work more hours for the causes she believed in, like reproductive rights, the intensity of her commitment to those causes grew stronger and has kept her going.

The topic of motherhood as a politically motivating experience isn't reserved for a handful of high-profile women on the national scene. Women all over America have found there are innumerable ways to become activists on issues that impact their lives in so many other ways. That's what happened when 29-year-old Krystal Ball gave birth to her daughter, Ella. The Virginia business owner and accountant wasn't a girl who dreamed of elective office or reveled in the political. But when she became a mother and thought about what kind of world she wanted to give her daughter, she became her own version of a Democratic "mama grizzly" by running for Congress.[42] Even though Ball ultimately lost to the Republican incumbent in her district, she made great strides on the road to using her mom voice to create political change, and has continued her political efforts by becoming a Democratic political strategist..

Filmmaker Amy Sewell of *Mad Hot Ballroom* fame, had her motherhood political "*A-ha*" moment when one of her twin daughters said she didn't think girls could ride motorcycles.[43] Her daughter explained she had never seen any girls, or women, tooling by on any two-wheeled vehicle other than a bicycle. In that moment, Sewell thought, "What else are my daughters *not* seeing that they think isn't possible?" And with that, the idea for her film *What's Your Point, Honey?* was born. To show her daughters—and all our daughters—what girls can achieve in the world, Sewell created a documentary about seven high school girls who wanted to put a new face on political leadership. Through the film, Sewell was able to show her own daughters her commitment to change and was able to give them many examples of girls showing girls that they have the power to change the world, just as much as boys.

Other mothers have experienced their "*a-ha*" moments in a variety of ways. California mother Victoria Rierdan Hurley discovered her moment of political inspiration when the budget at her son's school was repeatedly slashed.[44] Barack Obama's call for change during his 2008 presidential campaign inspired Hurley to become an advocate for bringing back the funds that had been axed, leaving her son's school with few resources for science and music classes, the library and other programs that she and other parents felt strongly should be a part of the school's curriculum.

As for activist Judith Stadtman Tucker, she says that after her family moved from a busy metropolitan area with many professional opportunities to a rural one with few job or child-care options, she found herself feeling cut off and disillusioned by the lack of opportunities for flexible employment for mothers. She was shocked and felt abandoned by her feminist sisters when it came to raising awareness about issues that negatively impacted mothers in the workplace, and felt compelled to create an online space to gather stories like hers in an effort to change that reality.

Tucker's experience of feeling that she'd become invisible in the working world inspired her[45] to create the *Mothers Movement Online,*[46] a site designed to advocate for increased social support for working mothers.

Examples of political mothers like these are much easier to find today with the rise of women's presence in the online world. As women have become the majority users of social media tools, they've become more engaged in the political world.[47] While not all of those women are mothers, women account for approximately 57 percent of Facebook users, 57 percent of Twitter users, and 64 percent of people on MySpace.[48] Fifty-three percent of those women are older than 40[49] and 80 percent of women over the age of 40 are mothers.[50] And when it comes to the blogosphere, reading or writing blogs is one of the most popular women's online activities in connection with social media. Consider all that with the fact that women make up more than 50 percent of American voters.[51] It doesn't take a graduate degree in math to see how much power and influence mothers really have.[52]

With the advent of these myriad online platforms, mothers across all professional and political spectrums are diving into the world of activism. And the women embracing these tools are quickly becoming political influencers.[53] Stephanie Himel-Nelson not only writes online more frequently about politics since the birth of her young sons, but she has also taken her activism into the offline world as the communications director of Blue Star Families, a non-partisan group of more than 12,000 with an online presence that advocates for issues that impact military families. In that role, Himel-Nelson, who also contributes to the group political site *MOMocrats,* helped launch the Blue Star Families 2010 Military Family Lifestyle Survey[54] at the first ever joint session of the Senate and House Military Family Caucuses. Himel-Nelson and BSF Research and Policy Director Vivian Greentree personally briefed the staff of the House Armed Services Committee on those survey results.

Other moms whose online presence was originally focused on the challenges of new motherhood quickly embraced the medium for social action. Kristen Chase, best known as one of the founders of the popular website *Cool Mom Picks,* as well as her irreverent personal blog *Motherhood Uncensored,* embraced her political side when she co-created the site *League of Maternal Justice.* The site addresses issues including recalls of dangerous toys, toxic plastics in baby bottles and sippy cups, and Facebook's ban on photos of breastfeeding mothers. Being an expert with online tools allowed Chase to branch out into a kind of activism that wasn't available just a few years ago.

In 2008, many news reports and government agencies dismissed efforts, like those of Chase, to call out manufacturers for the use of chemicals in products that babies and small children use every day. But by early 2010, the Food and Drug Administration, after years of denying there was a problem with chemicals, such as BPA, in plastics, finally admitted the existing danger to children , proving that the voices of activist mothers could change the world of bureaucratic politics.[55] After taking on Uncle Same and BPA manufacturers, Chase turned her attention to Facebook, when it announced it would ban photos of breastfeeding mothers, but still allow pictures to be posted of semi-nude women.

So why would a former academic and current blogger who's better known for sex advice and complaining about her in-laws jump into the world of online political activism to call out the FDA and social media giant Facebook?

"When Facebook banned photos of mothers breastfeeding their infants, something erupted inside of me and I decided that someone needed to send a...very public message that this was not right," Chase says. "I think what was so effective about the [Facebook campaign] was that it was not a bunch of stereotypical breastfeeding moms who were out there shaking their one free fist at a huge corporation," she continues. "It was taking something that many moms do every day at some point in their lives and making it media savvy—the images of superheroes with breast pumps. Giving it legs beyond a nurse-in was extremely effective."[56]

Chase and Himel-Nelson aren't the only women who've jumped into the online world to become activists on issues important to them as mothers. On the conservative side of the political aisle, Teri Christoph, a mother of four and co-founder of the site *Smart Girl Politics,* couldn't agree more with the idea of using a full arsenal of online tools to advocate for social and political change. Founded in November 2008, *Smart Girl Politics* was launched because Christoph and her co-founder Stacy Mott were frustrated with the 2008 presidential election outcome and wanted to find a way to promote a new conservative women's movement. Christoph was especially motivated by her concern about the potential financial burden she believed her children would face as adults because of federal government spending.

Smart Girl Politics quickly became a significant political player through its sponsorship of some of the first Tea Party rallies and the creation of its political activism conference Smart Girl Summit, which has attracted the interest of high-profile conservative women including Michele Bachmann, Michelle Malkin and Leslie Sanchez.[57]

On the political left, the progressive group blog *MOMocrats* was born when California blogging moms Glennia Campbell, Beth Blecherman, and Stefania Pomponi Butler met in a Palo Alto coffee shop in September 2007. They chatted about how fed up they were with the state of the country and George W. Bush's presidency. They were moved to take action and saw the potential of making their political voices heard in the social media world because they were already involved in other online projects. As these three moms with long histories of personal political activism sipped their lattes, the idea for creating a blog called *MOMocrats* was born.[58]

MOMocrats[59] quickly got noticed by the media and politicians[60] as one of the first group political sites written by women who self-identify as mothers, with the tag line "Raising the Next Generation of Blue." A group of *MOMocrat* contributors attended the Democratic National Convention in 2008 as credentialed media, and their site is frequented by progressive mothers looking for political commentary.

MOMocrats

As more mothers find others with similar philosophies, online political communities are growing and are now at the leading edge of creating new influential political actors. Community sites like *Moms-Rising* are giving increasingly higher profiles to mothers' activism and political mobilization. The goal of *MomsRising* is to focus lawmakers on issues that directly impact mothers and families and to create cultural and legislative change to benefit them, including paid maternity leave, paid sick leave, equal pay, and health care for all mothers and children.

Founded in 2006, *MomsRising* works with its members through e-mail petitions that voice their opinions and concerns about pending state and federal legislation. And if you're wondering whether even thousands of e-mail petitions can make a difference, the *MomsRising* website states, "*MomsRising* played a key role in securing paid family leave in New Jersey, Washington, and paid sick days in Milwaukee. Our efforts also helped pass legislation that removes highly toxic phthalates from young children's toys and products, and the Consumer Product Safety Reform Act that will better protect our families from toxic substances."

MomsRising started with about 40,000 members online and grew to about 200,000 members by mid-2009. Growing a membership base online takes time, but if an organization can make something go "viral" on the web, its following and political influence can explode overnight. That's exactly what happened for *MomsRising* when it combined established outreach methods, such as e-mail lists, with new online tactics. Its membership shot through the roof to more than one million over Mother's Day weekend in 2009,[61] as a result of a video it produced designed to honor mothers with a little personalized humor in a faux news report naming each recipient as Mother of the Year.

The still-amusing video introduced the concept of what online tools can do to advance a cause, attracting more engaged members to tap into for political action. *MomsRising* has used that increased membership and profile to move its online presence to the real world with offline action, such as visits to Capitol Hill.

Former White House Press Secretary Dee Dee Myers isn't surprised that more mothers are jumping into the political arena. In her 2008 book, *Why Women Should Rule the World,* Myers observed that for most women, motherhood becomes a pillar around which the rest of their lives are built, with every decision starting with the question of "How will it affect my children?" For Myers, that obviously includes the world of politics. When talking about the topic of why more mothers aren't seen as serious political actors, it's clear that this is an issue Myers is passionate about.

"Why is motherhood any less of a training ground for political participation?" Myers asked with a tone of dismay. "Why is it somehow less relevant than high school football and those lessons that so many men point to for their leadership experience? Really, what has more leadership experience—football or raising a family?"[62] The idea of leadership experience coming from being a mother was firmly embraced by Sarah Palin, who has been famously quoted as saying, "...there's no better training ground for politics than motherhood."[63]

As women have come together online, those in power have started taking more notice of women's political views and are reaching out to make connections with women influencers. At the large annual *BlogHer* writing and blogging conference in 2009, Valerie Jarrett, one of President Obama's most senior advisors, met with fifteen women bloggers (mostly mothers) to discuss the then-pending health care reform legislation to learn what concerns this group of engaged, connected women had about one of the most discussed and important topics of the day. As a result of some of the personal stories shared at that meeting, one of those women, Loralee Choate, who writes the popular blog *Loralee's Looney Tunes,* was invited to the White House by Jarrett to talk more about the health care and insurance problems she and her family have faced. As you can probably guess from her blog's humorous name, Loralee isn't a political writer by trade or an overly political person by nature. But she was able to turn a small moment for herself into one with a political impact far beyond a small meeting or a blog entry.

Similarly, Kim Moldofsky, founder of *MomImpact!* and author of the blog *Hormone-Colored Days* was invited by then-Speaker of the House Nancy Pelosi in March of 2010 to talk about the problems she had obtaining health insurance due to pre-existing health conditions at a press event for the health care debate.

Image by Meg Bohne, courtesy of Kim Moldofsky

In addition to being sought out by lawmakers, this increasingly influential motherhood power demographic is finally gaining some serious media attention. In a 2009 article in *Ms. Magazine,*[64] *Cyberhood Is Powerful: The Maternal Impulse Turns Political When You Mix Moms, Feminism, and the Blogosphere,* author Kara Jesella reported on the growing numbers of organizations and individuals embracing advocacy and feminism, using the lens of motherhood through which to focus their efforts. Jesella brought attention to the fact that even if we don't have the word "politics" in our blog names, the feminist mothers she interviewed who are engaging politically online are just the tip of the iceberg.

Other media outlets are slowly discovering that, as well. News networks are talking with mothers who write online to discuss the shaping of new programs.[65] Growing numbers of Congressmen and -women are hiring new media directors to reach out to women other than justbeyond those who post at well-known political blogs like *The Huffington Post, The Daily Caller, Firedoglake,* or the *Daily Kos.* With the following essays, and more to come online, there's no doubt that mothers are making inroads and wielding power in a wide variety of online communities. It won't be long until we have more influence on the world we leave to our children.

AN UNEXPECTED ALLY IN GLORIA STEINEM
by Julie Marsh, The Mom Slant blog

I may not call myself a feminist, but I recognize the primal role that Gloria Steinem played in the advancement of opportunities for women. I admire her initiative and leadership in the face of great opposition. So in spite of the differences in our political philosophies, I was thrilled when my friend invited me to attend a lunch at which Ms. Steinem was speaking.

Gloria Steinem is spending this last week before the election in Colorado, making appearances around the Denver metro area. But yesterday's lunch was a private one, held at a Denver home, and about a hundred women (and a few men) gathered in the backyard to hear Ms. Steinem.

While I was certainly excited to see this iconic woman in person, I was also a bit uncomfortable. I knew I'd be in the political minority—just as I am in the corner of the blogosphere where I spend most of my time—but I didn't know whether the atmosphere would be welcoming and accepting, or if it would have the same "us" versus "them" feel that the Elizabeth Edwards closing keynote speech at *BlogHer* '07 did (for me, at least).

Image by Julie Marsh, with permission

It didn't help my state of mind that on the way to the lunch, I saw this truck on I-25:

Is this what the Republican Party has come to? Is this what Democrats and Independents see—a truck that is literally wearing a sandwich board proclaiming the supremacy of the second amendment (which, by the way, Barack Obama supports) —as emblematic of the GOP?

Color me pleasantly shocked when Steinem brought up this same point in her talk—that the Republican Party has been taken over by extremists. That John McCain could have selected a female running mate to draw in the moderate Republicans who feel alienated by their party; instead, he selected a running mate with the goal of solidifying the support of that extremist faction.

I couldn't agree more. I was so hopeful at the outset of McCain's candidacy. Mike Huckabee and Mitt Romney had been cast aside by primary voters in favor of a man who wasn't part of that so-called base. Rush Limbaugh and Sean Hannity were incensed. Perhaps the party would start moving away from the religious right and the extreme social conservatism that had caused me to change my party affiliation.

But McCain let me down. He started pandering, and he hasn't stopped. I don't recognize him anymore.

I've been seriously considering voting for Bob Barr, the Libertarian Party candidate, even though I can't get the image of his appearance in the movie *Borat* out of my head. I'd vote for him not because I think he has a chance in hell of ever becoming president, but because I want to send a message that two choices are not enough.

Perhaps they could be though if the Republican Party could overcome the narrow cross-section of views that have come to represent the party as a whole.

I have many friends with whom I have philosophical differences. Those differences don't preclude friendship. But I do sometimes feel as if they are waiting for me to come to my senses. I wonder sometimes if their respect for me isn't lessened because I don't share their priorities.

But Ms. Steinem spoke so kindly and even-handedly, with respect and optimism, regarding the Republican Party and its members—people like my husband Kyle and me. For once, I didn't get the message that "Republican = Evil," a sentiment I hear daily on cable news and Twitter, even from people I like and who like me.

I went to this lunch for the opportunity to hear people speak from another perspective—one that I may not agree with fully, but which is worth consideration. I expected to feel like an outsider, especially in the presence of a liberal feminist icon. Instead, I felt compassion and understanding.

Ms. Steinem, thank you. For spending time in Denver, for the

opportunity to hear you speak, and for being an unexpectedly kind and understanding voice in a sea where I continue to swim against the currents.

She likes babies too. She said so.
Image from Julie Marsh, with permission

EXCUSE ME, SENATOR MCCAIN–WHAT I WANT FOR MY DAUGHTER ISN'T ABOUT BEING LIBERAL OR CONSERVATIVE
by Joanne Bamberger, PunditMom blog

As the mother of a daughter, there are things I want for my eight-year-old, especially when she becomes a woman–things that I was lucky to have, but that generations before me didn't. Interestingly, John McCain, as the father of daughters, doesn't seem to want those same things.

Since we are both parents of daughters, I'm a bit confounded, Senator McCain, about your lack of interest in things that would benefit your girls directly. I know you probably won't pay much attention, but here is the list of the things I want for my third-grader:

1. Equal pay for equal work. I know you seem to think that's all about more education and women working harder, but that's just nonsense and you know it. You just don't have the spine to stand up to your GOP colleagues and vote for something that should be every daughter's right in this country. Ask your daughters Meghan and Bridget; I'm betting they'd agree. Your oldest daughter Sidney, who's an executive in the music industry, might also have some really enlightening things to chat about when it comes to women in the workplace. You might want to sit down with her about that...soon.

2. To be a feminist. I know you think that "feminist" is a dirty word.

I could tell by the Dr. Evil smirk on your face when you told Chris Wallace on Fox News that Sarah Palin was a "direct counterpoint to the liberal feminist agenda for America." And then to support your comment, you referred to the fact that Palin is a mother and has a family, as if those things are at odds with being a feminist.

The funny thing is that the definition of a feminist is someone who advocates for the rights of women to be equal to the rights of men in all ways, including the social and political worlds. If you don't believe me, you can look it up in the dictionary.

Hmmm. That definition doesn't sound overly liberal to me. And Senator, you must be a feminist yourself because you apparently believe that Sarah Palin is as competent as you to be president. Otherwise, you would never have chosen her to be your running mate, right? Again, I'm thinking your daughters might have a few interesting thoughts on whether they think having equal rights is so horribly progressive.

3. Adequate paid maternity leave. You might be familiar with my reason for wanting this, because when my husband and I adopted our daughter, I was a federal employee—just like you! As a result, I did not get any paid leave, and it wasn't because we adopted to form our family. No federal employees get paid maternity leave, not even the parents who have their children the "old-fashioned" way. I know when you and your wife Cindy adopted your daughter Bridget, whether you got to take paid leave wasn't an issue : senators don't get docked pay for taking time off and, of course, even if you had, Cindy is financially loaded, so it wouldn't have been a problem for you. For us? It sure would have been helpful to have had even part of my paycheck for those six to eight weeks.

Since she's only in third grade, my daughter, PunditGirl doesn't have to make a decision yet about whether she wants to become a mother, but I know she wants to work at something, so it would be lovely if mothers in the future actually got some paid leave, like, say, the rest of the civilized world, so she won't have to worry.

4. Access to safe and affordable birth control. I was lucky. I came of age at just the right time in terms of having access to birth control. I'm particularly happy about that because without it, there's a big chance that my life would be a lot different today. You see, John, (may I call you John?), I made a pretty reckless decision and got married when I was a *very* young 19. The marriage didn't last long because it turned out that my now ex-husband was pretty abusive in a lot of ways. I am thankful every day that we didn't have any children that either would have tied me to him in some way for the rest of my life or would have been exposed to an abusive father. Without access to birth control, I shudder to think how things might have turned out differently.

The Bush administration you are so cozy with is still in its waning days doing everything it can to take that right away. That's not something I have to worry about so much anymore, but don't you and your conservative cronies dare take away from my daughter what she may want and need when she's a young woman. Again, maybe you've neglected to chat with your daughters about birth control and how they feel about this?

Senator McCain, those are just a few of the things I want for my daughter. They don't have anything to do with being a conservative or a liberal, no matter how you try to paint it. What I would like, though, is for you to wipe that 'I'm-so-far-behind-in-the-polls' smirk off your face when you hold Sarah Palin up as the shining example of anti-feminist, conservative motherhood.

'Cause you know, without feminism Palin couldn't even be your running mate.

A LETTER TO MY SONS: WHY I'M VOTING FOR BARACK OBAMA
by Stephanie Himel-Nelson, Lawyer Mama blog

Dear Hollis & Holden,

Tomorrow is November 4, 2008. That date doesn't mean much to you now, but I'm hoping that someday it will. You'll learn the date that the United States elected the John F. Kennedy of my generation.

It's hard for me to explain to you both, at three and four, just what this election means to me. All you know right now is that Mommy hasn't been home a lot and you wish I could put you to bed more often.

You see, once upon a time I was young and idealistic. I wanted to help people and change the world. But then I discovered that putting yourself out there can hurt, really hurt, when you fail. I became an armchair activist, donating money instead of my time, and talking and writing about social justice instead of taking action.

Then I had the two of you.

You see, voting isn't just about me and who I'll get to rant about for the next four years. Now my vote is about your future. I want the world you live in to be free from racism and hate. I want our country and our leaders to take the issue of poverty seriously and to listen to the people they govern.

It's not that I won't be able to give you the world. You two are incredibly lucky. You were born white to two educated, professional parents. We may tend to hover a bit, but we'll do whatever we have to do to make sure you get the best education and the best opportunities in life.

So why do I care so much? Because I want every other child in this country to have that as well.

When I became your mother, I became **A Mother**. When I see a child without a coat on in 30-degree weather I shiver for him and look around for a coat, just like his mother would. When I hear about a child harmed, I cry the tears her mother will. When I learn that 14 million children in this country don't have health insurance, I get pissed off and I want to change that, just like those 14 million mothers do.

I hope to teach both of you that we are all inextricably intertwined as human beings and Americans. We can't turn our heads and pretend we don't see the problems of others. I don't want you to grow up making excuses for your privilege and the poverty of others, attempting to justify a system of haves and have-nots.

You may work hard as a soldier or lawyer or accountant, but so do our trash collectors and our teachers and our plumbers. Yes, you will encounter people who don't work as hard as you, who can't hold a job, who have too many children and not enough money. But I want both of you to realize that you are no more entitled to the necessities of life than they are. You've just been very, very lucky through happy accident of birth.

Barack Obama, more than any public servant of my lifetime, seems to understand this and all that I want you to learn.

I didn't start out as a Barack Obama supporter. But as I've researched his policies, spoken with his wife, his vice presidential pick, and too many surrogates to name, I've become convinced that he is the perfect man to unite our divided country. And so, because I want to change our country, I got involved in a political campaign for the first time in my life.

It's not just me either. There are so many mothers and fathers and grandparents and students and first-time voters getting involved. They, like me, see something in Barack Obama that is different, that stands for hope and the promise of better things to come. I haven't seen people united in such a cause since the days after the 9/11 attacks, and that ended quickly enough. This time, I'm hopeful that people will stay involved. I'm hopeful that people will see that they *can* make a difference and that they *did* make a difference.

I'm hopeful that people will keep getting involved and keep trying to change the world and keep fighting for justice for all the other people that inhabit this country, this world, this third rock from the sun.

In what I believe will be one of history's most remembered speeches, Barack Obama reminded us all that we have to fight not for ourselves, but for others. He shared a story of a campaign organizer named Ashley, sharing why she'd gotten involved—because of what her mother had gone through when she got cancer and lost her insurance and her ability to support her family:

> *Anyway, Ashley finishes her story and then goes around the room and asks everyone else why they're supporting the campaign. They all have different stories and reasons. Many bring up a specific issue. And finally they come to this elderly black man who's been sitting there quietly the entire time. And Ashley asks him why he's there. And he does not bring up a specific issue. He does not say health care or the economy. He does not say education or the war. He does not say that he is there because of Barack Obama. He simply says to everyone in the room: "I am here because of Ashley."*

"I'm here because of Ashley." By itself, that single moment of recognition between that young white girl and that old black man is not enough. It is not enough to give health care to the sick, or jobs to the jobless, or education to our children.

But it is where we start. It is where our union grows stronger. And as so many generations have come to realize over the course of the 221 years since a band of patriots signed that document in Philadelphia, which is where the perfection begins.

It isn't enough for me to just feed and clothe and take care of the two of you, my boys. It may not be enough for me to vote, knock on doors, do interviews, write articles, and make phone calls to get Barack Obama elected. But it is where I, and so many others, start. We're doing it for you and all the other people in this country because "that is where the perfection begins."

That's my son Hollis on the right
Image by Heidi Kulberg, with permission
from Stephanie Himel-Nelson

Yes. Yes, we can.

Love,

Mommy

TO MY DAUGHTER, ON THE ELECTION
by Jessica Pieklo, Care2 blog

In a matter of hours life will change, again. And not just because of the election, but because I will have given birth to my daughter.

With her birth the day before the 2010 midterms, it has been impossible not to merge the two events in some fashion, which has led to a lot of reflection on the state of the world I'm bringing her into. As a feminist, I've fought hard for health-care reform but witnessed my own party throw me and my fellow women under the bus when it came to reproductive rights and access to safe, affordable health-care options.

So my daughter will enter a world where doctors are targets of political assassinations, where violence against women is so mainstream even campaign staffers engage in it with very little public condemnation, and a serious female political candidate still must address her wardrobe and hair as qualifications of leadership.

Despite significant advances in both the public and private sectors, my daughter will enter a world where the social safety net that emerged as a result of the Great Depression and that has been so very critical in helping lift and keep millions of women and children out of poverty is on the brink of being completely undone by, in large part, women who benefited from the security of minimum wages and child labor protections. These "Mama Grizzlies" call themselves feminists but campaign on a very platform antithetical to the interests of women. This will be her world.

My daughter will also enter a world where, despite an entire political party built upon values of "family," her father cannot take paid paternity leave because it's not offered by his employer and her mother will juggle the demands of work and home almost immediately after her birth to help pay for the portion of her birth that a private-industry insurance bureaucrat deemed "non-essential." And I'll do that juggling for about .28 cents less money that a man would. Still.

I wish I could say that my daughter is entering a world that is stronger, safer and more accepting of women than when I was born, but I don't think I can. But I *can* say that armed with that knowledge I fully intend to make sure that should my daughter decide to become a mother that answer will change. It has to. There's simply no other acceptable alternative.

WHEN AN EAR INFECTION MEANS BEING UNINSURABLE
by Sheila Bernus Dowd, MOMocrats blog

My kids and I were uninsured. I was frustrated, angry and felt utterly helpless because some insurance company gets to decide if I get back in the club—the "people who have insurance club." I never thought our family would be the uninsurable kind, and here's why.

I am a soccer mom and PTA president; I am caretaker for both my children and my ailing father-in-law. I live in Silicon Valley and like many, my husband and I are entrepreneurs and small-business owners. Like the Google guys Brin and Page or Hewlett and Packard, we literally started our small high tech consulting business out of our home office in our garage. While we created our business plan carefully, one thing we had not planned on was the cost of health care and its impact on our lives.

My husband and I have been fortunate enough to always have been provided with group insurance through our employers. Thus, as we made the transition to being self-employed, we had a state COBRA plan from a previous employer, which included dental and vision coverage—expensive, yet comprehensive. After our mortgage, paying for health care ($1,500 a month) was our largest expense each month. Being proactive and committed to building our own business, I began the search to purchase an individual or family health plan. The rates were high, so we opted to apply for plans with high deductibles and lower monthly rates.

I was shocked. I had no idea that this opened us up to something called "pre-existing conditions." At the time, I thought that meant having a serious disability or a type of cancer. For our family, in fact, it meant a toddler with ear infections, pollen allergies and a running injury. I thought we were a healthy family—we are a healthy family—and that buying "basic" health insurance would be a snap. But as a result of having a child who suffered from the slightest of normal childhood conditions, most health plans we looked at deemed us "uninsurable."

We were denied insurance coverage outright twice. After relentlessly calling our family doctors to petition the denial and calling the insurance company every day, we finally secured a health plan. The insurance company called this "catastrophic" insurance—the kind you have in case of an emergency. You buy it because you are a responsible parent and while you can't really afford it, you need it because your son could break a leg playing soccer or your daughter might unexpectedly need antibiotics. An appendectomy.

Our insurance nightmare woke me up. It made me realize that my job as a mother required far more than kissing boo boos and making dinner. It required me to be an advocate for my family and kids in a whole new way—to understand the system and how to leverage my resources. It clarified for me that my story was not uncommon and that if I didn't speak out, I didn't know who would. While I had been blogging for years, I had never stood in front of people, in the wake of protesters and shared my personal struggles. Yet, that is exactly what I did.

I educated myself on the plans being discussed in Washington, D.C. I gave testimony to our local Congresswoman about my family's struggle, I gave radio and television interviews and wrote about our family's experience on blogs, like MOMocrats. I shared our story in the hope that others would do the same and or that someone would help us find a solution.

When my friends asked me to speak at a health insurance rally outside Congresswoman Zoe Lofgren's office, I didn't hesitate to volunteer. But as I watched the news and read online accounts of what was happening at rallies around the country during the summer of 2009, I began to wonder what I had gotten myself into. Moreover, when the head organizer mentioned that agitators were seen at other rallies around the country and that a large group of Tea Party members assembled at an event the night before, I began to worry about what I had gotten my kids involved with. But as I stood in a circle that day, sharing a story I never thought would happen to my mostly healthy family, I was surrounded by preachers, community activists and friends, and I knew there was no other place I would rather have been.

We are lucky to have health insurance now. It isn't great, but we have it and I can go to soccer games without worries that we might go bankrupt because of a broken bone or injury. The system must change and this mama is doing everything she can to bring this same peace of mind to other mamas across the country.

OPEN LETTER TO SCHOLASTIC BOOK FAIR
by Liza Barry-Kessler, LizaWasHere blog

Dear Scholastic VP Responsible for the Book Fair:

It is Saturday night. I was supposed to spend this evening watching trash TV, eating a take-out frozen custard sundae, and relaxing.

Instead, that frozen custard is churning in my stomach, and I'm trying to decide how badly my three-and-a-half-year-old son will feel when I tell him that we have to return his new Bakugan and Life Size Dinosaur books because they came from a company that doesn't want people to know that families like his exist.

I'm talking, of course, about your outrageous effort to tell author Lauren Myracle to change her new book *Luv Ya Bunches* so that one of the characters no longer has lesbian moms.

You see, I am a lesbian mom, and I am also the co-chair of my school's Scholastic Book Fair.

I feel positively sick that I have spent time and energy supporting a company that doesn't want authors to expose children to my family or to deal with the irritation of occasional homophobic individuals complaining that their children might learn that two-mom (or two-dad) families exist.

I hope I can find new copies of the books I bought my son somewhere else, so that I can return the ones we bought at the book fair when it re-opens on Monday. And I am making a list of independent bookstores to contact about helping us with next year's book fair.

I understand you are still willing to list *Luv Ya Bunches* in the Scholastic Book Club catalog, just not the book fair. It isn't the same thing and it isn't good enough. With book fair books, children, parents, and teachers pick up the books and look at them. Almost no one leaves a book fair with no books.

In fact, because so many of the kids are drawn to books with television or cartoon characters, even as their parents are drawn to classics or beautifully illustrated stories, many families make multiple purchases from the book fairs. Teachers list these books on their wish lists, and parents donate them to classrooms. In other words, book fair books get much more exposure than catalog books.

And my family deserves to have the kind of casual, ordinary exposure that *Luv Ya Bunches* provides.

THE STRUGGLES OF A REPUBLICAN ON THE FENCE
by Dana Tuszke, The Dana Files blog

Eight years ago, if you had asked me why I love politics, I would have replied with many wonderful reasons.

I would have told you that if you never vote, you have no right to complain about the state of our country's government. I would have said that we are responsible for changing the things we dislike about government. I would have encouraged you to vote and help others get out and vote. I may have even talked about the American Dream and the dreams my great-grandparents brought with them on their way to Ellis Island from the war-torn country of Poland.

Ask me the same question today and the answer would be completely different. As time has gone by, I've loved politics less and less. I've become cynical about our government, the politicians who claim to serve "We the people," and the motives of the Democrat and Republican Parties. I don't know if I believe in "the American Dream" anymore.

As a lifelong Republican, I have looked at this country through a different lens than most others, and over the years I've become disheartened with every broken promise, every scandal, every downright lie that has been told to the American people. I can't entirely blame George W. Bush, for he has Congress and advisors pushing and pulling him in various directions, but I do believe that his priorities have been mixed up.

When the United States first entered this war in Iraq, I was upset. My reasons were selfish. I didn't want my brother and sister, members of the National Guard, to be sent to the Middle East. I didn't want them, or anyone else, to risk their lives for what I believed was an impossible cause.

Yet, I was angry that terrorists had claimed the lives of nearly 3,000 innocent people on September 11th. As a Catholic, it pains me to confess that I believed that Osama bin Laden needed to be punished, even killed.

And so, I looked away. We sent thousands of troops overseas, far away from their families, and I convinced myself that we were on the right path, that soon this war would be over. It was so naive to think that way.

As I watched the news, day after day, seeing reports of more in-nocent military men and women dying in a useless war, I became sad. I felt remorse. I felt ashamed. Even though I was so honored by and proud of our troops, the ones who have acted selflessly for this coun-try, I was sickened for even thinking we were doing the right thing.

I watched as this war went from being "The Avenging of 9/11" to "The Obsessive Hunt for Saddam Hussein" and no longer about end-ing terrorism. I began to wonder what the hell our troops were doing there in the first place. I felt lied to by President Bush and every mem-ber of Congress that voted in favor of sending our troops to Iraq.

Inevitably my brother Nathan was deployed to Kuwait for 17 months. Even though he wasn't on the front lines, I worried about his safety every single day. When he finally returned home, he was no longer my little brother.

He was a man. He grew up. He became hardened by the things he experienced.

He was a man who served for... I don't know what. Our coun-try? Our government? Me? You? Iraqi freedom? Honestly, what are the troops fighting for?

When my son grows up, will he ever be in a war? I pray to God the answer is no. But how do I know? There's no way to answer that question.

As a mother, I look at my son and I think about the world he has to grow up in. A world filled with tragedy, violence, poverty. A world of uncertainty. What does the future hold for my children? Will my son have his own American Dream?

With the 2008 election progressing every day, I've been im-mersed in the issues of foreign policy, the war, the economy, health care, immigration, abortion, education, poverty, the environment, maternal rights, domestic violence, and more. My list is endless. And each time I think about it, I think of the future and what prob-lems my children will inherit.

Will troops still be stationed in Iraq 20, 30 or 50 years from now? John McCain admits this is a possibility, almost a certainty. He's prepared for 100 years in the Middle East. Will women finally be paid fairly and equally for doing the same jobs as men? Hillary Clinton assures us she will fight for this important issue.

Will our country find hope and inspiration and trust in the government again? Barack Obama pledges to bring Americans together for the greater good. Will Americans finally receive the health-care benefits they so desperately need? Will all human life be respected and protected, even the unborn? Can Democrats and Republicans work together to make the government work for everyone?

In spite of all the unanswered questions and uncertainties, I believe it's imperative that we work together. We must stay abreast of political issues and come together to turn this country around. *This is the most important issue.*

Together, *we can* make America the great country that it once was, a country we are proud to live and work in. This is my new American Dream, and it's the reason I've fallen in love with politics again. What is your American Dream?

A LETTER TO WALL STREET FROM A MOM
by Amie Adams, Mamma Loves .... blog

Dear Failed Wall St. Financial Executives,

We need to talk about your behavior.

There are rules we all live by—rules my three boys must follow in our house. I'm betting your parents enforced them in your homes, too. We didn't make up these rules so we could find excuses to take away your privileges. We created these rules so that you would grow up to be law-abiding, contributing members of society, so you could make and keep friends and so we could actually take you out of the house without being completely embarrassed.

See the thing is, my children who are still quite young, are having an easier time behaving than you seem to be. Your lying and inability to make responsible decisions can no longer be tolerated.

Millions of people have lost vast amounts of money because of your actions. Bills will go unpaid, causing other businesses to suffer. Those about to retire may now be looking at additional years of work when they should be enjoying the plans they had for their money that is now gone. Children will receive fewer presents this coming holiday season. Families will cancel vacations.

Your bad behavior affects not only you but hundreds of millions of people, too.

When my kids misbehave, they must face the consequences. How am I going to explain to them that when YOU misbehave the consequences aren't yours to face, but theirs?

I haven't decided yet what your punishment should be. I need time to consider it when I'm not so angry. In the meantime, you need to go sit in the corner and think about your actions. I'll call you when I'm ready to talk—in about fifty years.

Love,

Mamma

COULD OBAMA-ISM BE THE OPIATE OF THE MASSES?
by Jessica Gottlieb, Jessica Gottlieb blog

In September 2008, the stock market went into a free fall. While AIG got a bailout and Lehman Brothers filed for bankruptcy, Los Angelenos went to a fundraiser in an historic Beverly Hills mansion. The privileged spent time with presidential candidate Barack Obama and 300 of their closest friends. People were losing their jobs, their retirements, their homes and their dreams; but not Obama supporters, they had faith that there would be *change*.

Tickets for the party? $28,500 each. No, that wasn't a typo. The cost of shaking hands with the Democratic Party nominee (and allegedly still a member of the Senate, though I saw no proof of that) for a party of two was a whopping $57,000. Can someone please explain to me how an ill-timed elitist Hollywood fundraiser held during out nation's darkest fiscal failures is revolutionary?

It's the cult of Obama. Nothing about it made sense. People changed their social networking pictures to Obama's face. For several months, I simply had to remove those people from my networks. It's not that I didn't like those folks. I adored many of them, and I love diverse voices. The constant Obama issue gave me the heebie jeebies; it was as though otherwise smart and rational people had ceased thinking and joined a massive cult.

At the time I remember being curious as to how Barack Obama was going to use the $5.6 million raised at one dinner party.

I wondered if Barack Obama would pay the legal fees for the kid who hacked Sarah Palin's personal e-mail? I wondered if he would buy more advertising. Perhaps they could have run a campaign wherein people were reminded that he had a running mate with a pulse. During the campaign there were curiously few mentions of Joe Biden.

I loved that the Obama campaign called for change, but did any-one notice that Joe Biden was deeply embedded in Washington, D.C. cronyism? Did anyone know what they were getting with Biden? Biden has been in the Senate almost as long as I've been alive; does that sound like change to you? Did anyone care any longer?

I knew what Obama would do with the money. He'd invest in a little more negative campaigning, wherein he'd blast John McCain for having married an (insanely) wealthy woman. You see, someone with a few homes is automatically not down to earth enough for the Democratic Party. In order to run for office, one must be perfectly average. Salt of the earth even.

Accepting $57,000 for two adults to attend a dinner party is insan-ity. It was elitism at its worst. I love Hollywood; we live in a house that TV built. Clearly, I wanted our president to be media friendly. Where's the dividing line though? Media friendly versus media sycophant?

Which brings me to the point of all of this.

The advertising and the ridiculousness of Obama's face *every-where* was, frankly, annoying. Not a little bit annoying either. We are Americans, we don't have kings and queens, we don't have presidents we revere. We have presidents that we hold account-able through checks and balances. We have presidents and vice presidents that we employ and reserve the right to fire.

So please understand that the now-famous pop art Shepard Fairey campaign posters of an inspirational skyward-looking Barack Obama that was plastered everywhere reminded me, and not in a good way, of the infamous political propaganda images used so successfully by Mao Tse-Tung as political messiah iconography. We might need change, but we don't need a messiah.

HOW VOMIT CAN INSPIRE WOMEN TO VOTE
by Caroline Jorgensen, Morningside Mom blog

Apparently women are too tired and fed up to vote. No really, that's what they are saying. We are so sad about how badly things are going that we have shrugged our shoulders and given up on tomorrow's election. Our expected apathy has GOP- and Tea Party-goers giddy and relaxed. If we don't show, if we don't rally like we did in the 2008 Presidential election, they have this election in the bag.

Now here is where I am going to talk about how a vomiting little boy has inspired this post.

The night before Halloween, my seven-year-old stumbled out of his room in a cold sweat, climbed into my lap on the couch and proceeded to upchuck his entire ravioli dinner all over my t-shirt. And it didn't end there. He spent the rest of the night heaving into a bowl while curled next to me on my towel-draped bed. The following morning, Halloween morning, he managed to power down some ice chips. But then his ashen face faded from gray to blazing pink. He had spiked a 103-degree fever. And trick or treating would begin in less than six hours.

So what happened? My son dug deep. He had faith that his parents had the answers. He believed with all his might that if he pushed himself to hydrate and took that nasty ibuprofen Mommy had hovering in front of him, he would somehow get better.

Clearly, a surge of adrenaline and his crazed little-boy drive to run door to door for candy in his X-ray skeleton costume had lit a fire within. By the time the sun had set, he was fever free, jumping gleefully around the house and ready to give it all he had.

Predictably, after an incredible night of house-to-house antics, my son collapsed into bed at nine o'clock. His fever had returned but, with a plastic pumpkin overflowing with Skittles and Smarties and his costume crumpled in the bedroom corner, he was victorious.

We need a little of what my son had yesterday.

According to all kinds of polls rating how depressed and apathetic women are regarding this election, we are supposed to be staying home tomorrow. No election trick-or-treating for us. No sir. We will accept our pathetic, fevered, rather ill situation. We give up.

Studies are showing that when men get angry, they go do something. But when women get angry, they get super sad. And turn inward. And do… nothing.

Nothing?!

One woman was quoted in the *Huffington Post* as saying she doesn't know where to turn now. There aren't any real answers to our problems. And the financial issues are just… beyond us.

Um, ok. So let's just stay home and do nothing.

Look, I get it. Do I have any flipping clue about how to fix our economy? Not so much. Am I feeling a little disillusioned by politics after seeing a Democratic majority do so very little with what they had? Hell yeah. And does it make me ill to watch political commercial after political commercial use the term "Obama liberal" like a four letter word? *Shudder* Yes.

So fine. Sometimes I just want to pretend our economy hasn't gone to hell. Sometimes I want to completely ignore that more focus is being put on stopping our administration than working with it towards a constructive compromise. Sometimes I'd rather just tell cute stories about my kids, bake and be a mom.

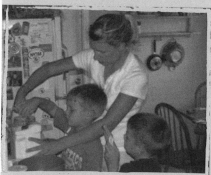

Image courtesy Caroline Jorgensen

Sometimes.

But it's not time to do nothing. Not now. Because I can bake and read *Harry Potter* to my kids and vote and care about my country all at the same time. Because women are multi-taskers. And we are smart. And we make a difference.

And women will not just stay home and pout about the state of our union. We won't say we don't feel so good about what's going on. We won't just—oh fiddlesticks, this politics thing is a pain in the ass, I'm going to go clip coupons—give up.

Like my son had faith in hydration and Motrin, we need to have faith that our vote will count. And our vote can make change happen, I swear to you. It takes time but we can affect change.

Don't believe me?

Women make up 51 percent of the population and 54 percent of voters—closer to 60 percent if measuring Democratic voters alone.

We need to show them. We need to show them that we are mad. We have had it. And we aren't going to stay home and fold socks and internalize our worries because we don't want to cause any trouble.

We need to show them we have power and we can stand up for what we deserve.

Don't make these polls right. Don't ignore and be passive and not care.

Vote. VOTE DAMMIT.

DO SOMETHING.

THE SUPREME COURT DOESN'T NEED ANOTHER MOM
by Sasha Brown-Worsham, The Stir by CafeMom blog

Supreme Court nominee Elena Kagan has no children and according to **Michael Roston**, a writer for *True/Slant*, this is going to mean the difference between a caring, loving Supreme Court and a heartless Darth Vader-like court bent on worldwide destruction.

OK, that last piece may be an exaggeration.

But seriously, Roston does make the argument in his May 9 essay that Kagan represents the end of an era of motherhood on the Court and that this is a bad thing, indeed.

Roston says:

> *"To me, if a woman doesn't have a child, she has only an abstract ability to pass judgment on issues where motherhood is concerned. I say this not out of disrespect for childless women, whose own struggles I would not dare to play down. Rather, I say it out of respect for all the mothers in the world, including my own. Women with the concrete knowledge of the decision-making that comes with motherhood simply know better ... 'A mother knows best' as we so often say."*

I really, really want to love this. I really do. After all, I'm a mother and my fellow mamas hold a special place in my heart. But try as I might, I can't shake the sense that no one would say this about a man.

I've never once heard anything about a man's fatherhood status having an effect on his ability to make decisions or advance in his career. And although I recognize that Roston is speaking in more of a general way about the Court and not calling out Kagan herself, it does ring a bit uncomfortable, as though we women are nothing more than our ovaries with some brains stuffed in as an afterthought.

I know many "childless" women who are just as capable of empathy as those who have given birth. And I also know many cold, heartless, horrible women who have given birth. I don't think our ability to procreate has much of an effect on our ability to empathize.

I also think there's a fair amount of hypocrisy in the idea that a woman without a child can't make decisions "where motherhood is concerned." Haven't men without wombs been making those decisions for years? What about a woman who can't bear a child? Is she less able to comment on matters that have to do with motherhood just because her body is unable to produce a child?

Dangerous ground, I say. And so when Roston says (channeling Gloria Steinem):

> *"I must insist that a Supreme Court without a mother on the bench would be as incomplete as a tricycle with two wheels. Mothers make the world move forward, and they need to have a voice in the arrangement of our society, from the boardroom to the courtroom and beyond."*

I want to agree. I really do. I believe in motherhood. I believe it has made me a stronger person who's much more capable than I ever was before. But I don't think we need a mother (or for that sake, a father) on the Supreme Court in order to make it effective.

I just don't see how the status of a person's womb is relevant to her ability to make effective decisions.

THE SUPREME COURT NEEDS ANOTHER MOM
by Joanne Bamberger, PunditMom blog

I'm not going to mince words: The Supreme Court needs another mom. Not the kind that'll make Clarence Thomas a peanut butter and jelly sandwich or remind John Roberts to clean his room. What the Supreme Court needs is more of a mother's perspective.

Don't get me wrong. I'm happy that President Obama nominated another woman to the Supreme Court with his selection of Solicitor General Elena Kagan. It sure will be nice to see three people in that annual "get-out-the-good-judicial-robe" photo who look sort of like me.

Interestingly though, after Justice John Paul Stevens announced his impending retirement, some columnists started writing about this crazy idea that maybe, just maybe, the Supreme Court nominee to replace Stevens ought to be a mother!

My response?

What I said!

Because when President Obama nominated Sonia Sotomayor to the high court last year, there was a short list of about half a dozen women he was considering. At the time I penned a post called *"The Supreme Court Needs a Mom."* In that post, I wrote:

> *Justice Ruth Bader Ginsburg has fought the good fight, especially with the language of her dissenting opinions, in calling out her fellow justices in their attitudes toward women, but she's only one vote. And she's 76. She needs some back-up.*

> *I'd like to suggest that a mother who still has children at home (or isn't too far out from that experience) could provide an interesting peek into the intersection of judicial ivory towers and real life—someone who is still living the daily reality of what it means to be the one in the family who brings home the bacon, fries it up in the pan, and makes sure the grease doesn't get poured down the*

sink because she'll be the one who has to take time off from work when the plumber has to come and snake the drain. Someone like that could be a powerful voice of reason when it comes to getting the remaining members of the Supreme Court to remember that there is a place for the law to intersect with real life.

In raising the question this time around, one writer at the blog *Jezebel* asks, "Does it really matter if the woman nominated is a mother?"

In a word: yes. A woman who also knows the realities of being a working mom and, most likely, has made less money at some point in her life than her male counterparts would have brought a perspective to the Lilly Ledbetter case that might have changed the outcome for her. Sure, President Obama signed the Ledbetter Act into law a couple of years later, but that didn't get Lilly any of the $365,000 in back pay and benefits that her employer should have paid her.

A woman who's faced issues with pregnancy complications— or who has sisters or friends who've dealt with the same things— could have been a powerful voice that might have convinced some others that there's more than one way to look at late-term abortions.

Many Republicans scoffed during the Sotomayor confirmation hearings about the role that our personal experiences play when it comes to applying the law. But laws don't exist in a vacuum. Often, laws have to be interpreted because believe it or not, there's nuance and subtlety to many statutes. If there wasn't, we wouldn't need lawyers or judges or a Supreme Court. Without relying on our personal experiences and stories, there's no context for interpretation or application of the law.

And that's why I say the Supreme Court needs another mom. Because I know the lens through which I viewed things like gender discrimination, reproductive rights, and a whole host of other issues did change after I became a mother. Things that happened to me after I had a child have impacted my perspective—and I'd like someone on the Supreme Court to be looking at cases about those issues who's had some of the same experiences I have.

It's not really just the Supreme Court we're talking about here. It's all high-powered professions and appointed government positions that still sorely lack any critical mass of mothers of young children in their ranks. I'd like to see some moms' perspectives there, too, say like in the House of Representatives. And the Senate. And the president's Cabinet.

Alas, it's not to be this time around for SCOTUS. I'm really not crazy when I say the Supreme Court needs another mom. After all, didn't your mother usually have good reasons for her decisions?

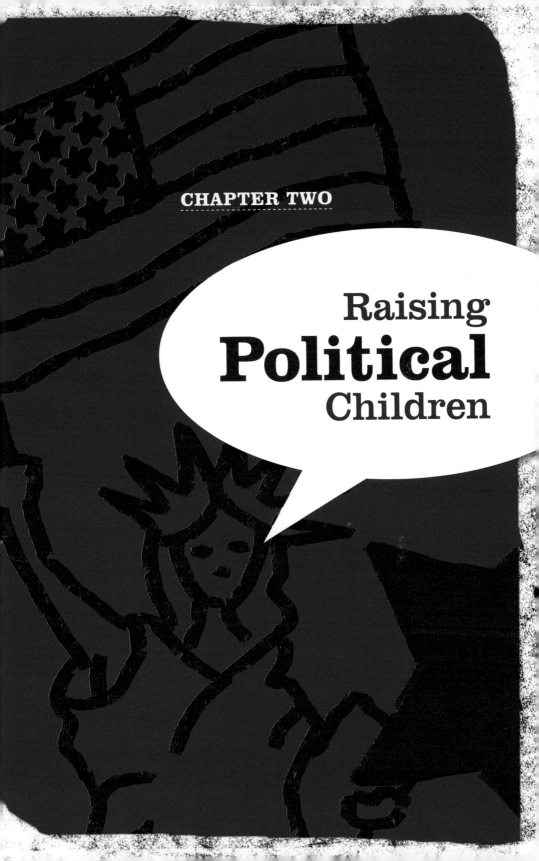

CHAPTER TWO

Raising **Political** Children

Nothing gets us mothers more stirred up than issues that have a direct impact on our children. We universally agree on most of the basics—keeping our children safe from harm, making sure they're warm in the winter and finding ways to slip more vegetables into their diets. When it comes to more advanced child-rearing, the level of disagreement widens as the topic moves further afield—at what age is it OK for our kids to ride their bikes around the block alone? How old should my daughter be before she's allowed to read *Harry Potter* or *Twilight?* Are you a bad mother if your son eats crackers containing high fructose corn syrup? How soon should we expose our children to the rough and tumble world of politics?

While some of these issues are the stuff that the so-called mommy wars are made of, there's usually an acceptable range of responses to parenting questions, even when mothers don't see eye-to-eye. Not so with partisan politics. Political engagement for kids isn't limited anymore to dressing them in T-shirts or baby onesies for candidates or to passing political references in kids' movies.[66] In the age of super-partisan politics, parents increasingly are taking an active role in molding their children in their own political images.[67]

A prime example of this new, hyper-activist level of political parenting occurred in 2009. The White House announced in late August that year that President Barack Obama would give a back-to-school pep talk on the importance of studying hard and staying in school, which would be broadcast live to schools around the country. After the text of the speech and accompanying teachers' materials were released, it's no understatement to say that all hell broke loose.

What seemed like a relatively straightforward, apolitical moment to many Americans caused some vocal parents to complain that their children were being exposed to political messaging they didn't want them to hear, causing some to cry, "*FOUL!*"[68] Even though the speech focused on students taking responsibility for homework, studying and graduating from high school, some conservative parents suggested that the president was going to use the speech to indoctrinate children with purportedly socialist messages about health care, increasing taxes, and higher national debt,[69] giving birth to a nationwide effort to keep children home from school that day to prevent them from hearing the speech.[70]

General outrage over the president's education remarks mounted when conservative commentators added fuel to the partisan fire. Right-wing pundit Michelle Malkin suggested the speech was intended to turn schoolchildren into "little lobbyists."[71] *Fox News* personality Glenn Beck told his radio listeners that the president's speech was an effort to indoctrinate children to the political left.[72] Even as President Obama's speech was defended by education advocate and former First Lady Laura Bush,[73] numerous vocal conservatives claimed that parents had a right to be upset because proposed Department of Education lesson plans suggested that students might have a discussion after the speech about whether they had been inspired by the president—a Democrat—claiming that the accompanying lesson plans "crossed the line between instruction and advocacy."[74]

After analyzing the speech and its lesson plans that drew the protest, *Politifact*, a site that fact-checks political claims by candidates and pundits, awarded the conservatives' contentions about Obama's speech a "Pants on Fire" rating on their Truth-o-Meter scale. In trying to put the episode in context, *Politifact* also pointed out that Presidents George H.W. Bush and Ronald Reagan had given similar speeches directly to schoolchildren in during their presidencies, causing some Democrats at the time to object.[75]

Regardless of which side of the argument surrounding President Obama's first-day-of-school address sounded more reasonable, it's fair to say that conservatives' calls for children to skip school in order to avoid the president's speech was a new political tactic, one that sent a clear message to children and politicians alike about what views parents want their kids exposed to and just how far they'd go to push their agenda.

In discussing this conservative groundswell over President Obama's speech, I asked in a *BlogHer* post, "[W]ith the economy still in the tank and getting worse,...two wars, health care hanging by a thread, and children going hungry every night,...isn't this a mole hill? It sure doesn't look like the Grand Tetons to me." Josette Crosby Plank, author of *Halushki* blog, countered with a more reasoned explanation for those who didn't want their children to hear the Obama speech:

> It isn't a mole hill if this is what gets people riled up. To discount... people's passion for this...event is to throw away just that momentum of energy, maybe just to prove a sour point. This was important to people. This got quite a few people who aren't usually politically active to write to their schools and take other action.
>
> . . . . . .
>
> Here's my main beef, and I feel like I'm getting blue in the face saying it: You, me, others...it's OK to say that we're OK with our kids hearing any messages from any political figure (which is, unfortunately, what the president has been boiled down to these days...) because we have the time and resources to help our kids look at it critically, look at the meta-questions raised, understand the rhetoric and how it effects them, etc. That this was an otherwise benign speech (as most all agree now) is of no consequence. When kids don't have those resources at home to learn critical thinking or when teachers don't have time and resources to concentrate on critical thinking skills, well, then any message becomes a threat. Huck Finn becomes a threat. Big Bang becomes a threat. Adam and Eve become a threat.

So when it comes to politics and our children—especially young children—if some parents believe a presidential stay-in-school-and-work-hard talk is off limits, or that children of Republicans shouldn't be asked to think about what they can do to "help" a Democratic president, then what *is* fair game and who should be doing the talking? Do we bring our kids into our respective political worlds by exposing them only to the political leanings we have as their parents? Or should our children's political awareness arise more naturally out of how we live our lives, exposing them to differing points of view and allowing them to come to political conclusions on their own?

The spectrum is wide in terms of how parents introduce the political world to their children. Different parents come to various conclusions and for some it's more than just taking our young children into the voting booth on Election Day. For some families, discussing subjects that fall under the broad category of "politics" is something of an organic process. When Stephanie Himel-Nelson's five-year-old son saw her give a homeless veteran five dollars while they were stopped at an intersection in the family car, she discovered that her son wanted to help as well. But that meant having the hard conversation with her kindergartner about why the man was homeless.

"I wasn't sure how much of our conversation he really followed," said Himel-Nelson, "but he surprised me when, after a few minutes of quiet thinking, he asked if he could give the man some of the money from his piggy bank." Ultimately, the homeless man wasn't at that intersection when they returned later, but Himel-Nelson went online with her son to contribute twenty dollars to an organization that targets veterans dealing with issues of mental illness, substance abuse, and homelessness.

Filmmaker Amy Sewell isn't entirely sure what impact her movie about girls and politics, *What's Your Point Honey?*, ultimately had on the political awareness of her own fourth-grade twin daughters, but they knew that their mom was working on a movie about young women who wanted to use the political process to help change the world. At the time of the movie's release, one of her daughters felt empowered enough to start a protest in her school yard because the boys wouldn't let the girls play stick ball. "She stole the stick and began marching around the yard, creating a girl conga line, chanting, 'Equal rights for women!'" says Sewell. "I picked her up that day to major kudos from fellow moms."

For parents who want to put a little more planning into their children's political education, children's books are plentiful. Books that can introduce our school-aged kids to the political world include historical and semi-biographical books like *First Kids, My Senator and Me: A Dog's Eye View of Washington, D.C.,* by the late Senator Ted Kennedy, *Barack Obama: Son of Promise, Child of Hope,* and *My Dad, John McCain.* Of course, our children can also get an introduction to politics by watching the classic *Schoolhouse Rock* television series that includes episodes entitled, *I'm Just a Bill, Sufferin' til Suffrage* and *Three-Ring Government.*

But some children's books are taking on a more highly partisan tone as a result of the increasing political divide that's developed over the last few years among Democrats, Republicans, Independents and, now, the "Tea Party." For example, one book—*Help! Mom! There Are Liberals Under My Bed!*—starts out as a story about two brothers who decide to open a lemonade stand to save up money to buy a swing set. Their plans are foiled, however, by one politician character who dashes their hopes by taxing the stand's profits and by another, who looks an awful lot like Hillary Clinton, who outlaws the sugary drinks they're trying to sell.

While some may regard books like *Help! Mom! There Are Liberals Under My Bed!* as political satire meant for the amusement of adults, author Katharine DeBrecht, who bills herself at her website as a political commentator and Fox News contributor, said in one online interview that the idea for the books first arose during the 2000 election season when she was trying to explain to one of her sons the difference between being conservative and being liberal.[76] Other books in her conservative education for children repertoire include the recent, *Help! Mom! Radicals are Ruining my Country!,* which stars a Sarah Palin-like heroine.[77] But political conservatives aren't the only ones getting in on the children's books as political fodder. At a site called *Little Democrats,* you can pick up books like *Why Mommy Is a Democrat, Why Daddy Is a Democrat* and *Mama Voted for Obama..* And both parties are starting to cater to the barely-old-enough-to-read crowd with coloring books about the Tea Party and Barack Obama.

These books can be light entertainment to adults who take them with a big grain of salt, but whether such openly partisan books can or should influence children's political education is another question. In her 2007 *Washington Post* editorial "Raising a Political Bigot,"[78] *New York Times* writer Catherine Rampbell examined the phenomenon of these books that seem aimed at instilling political talking points in our children rather than teaching them to be critical thinkers. She wondered if perhaps we should be worried about creating a generation of mini-partisans and what it says about parents who read these books to their children:

> These books are illustrative of a broader post-September 11 cultural directive: claim righteousness through some label (political, religious, or racial), and vilify anyone who doesn't identify with that label, regardless of any common concern for the human condition. The political climate beckoning our generation is eerily reminiscent of late-19th-century politics; back then, party organs ruled, and Americans often rooted for a political team whose only accepted definition was "not them."

No matter the resources in today's vitriolic political climate, it is a parenting challenge to strike the right balance between conveying the political values and ideas that are important in one's family while at the same time teaching our children that those with differing political views shouldn't be discounted. It's something we face in my family.

As two long-time Democrats, my husband and I want our daughter to understand why we believe what we believe, but we also want to teach her to respect our country's leaders, appreciate the idea that people we respect or love can have different views from our own, and that when she's an adult, she should come to her own conclusions about the world based on facts and the inferences she'll learn to draw from them.

In 2004, when she was only five years old, talking with our daughter generally about respecting people's different ideas worked well enough— there were plenty of playground analogies upon which to draw. But things got a bit more complicated in the political discussion department in 2008. My husband and I initially supported different presidential candidates during the primary election season. Our daughter, then in third grade, was shocked that we didn't agree from the start. She wanted more information about why we didn't support the same candidate.

We had many discussions at the dinner table and in the car to and from school about that difference of opinion. While I also toyed with the idea of finding ways to show her how to volunteer and support a candidate, it was tough to make that happen when Mommy and Daddy weren't initially on the same page about who to vote for.

Plenty of families did choose 2008 as the year to take their children door-to-door campaigning for the candidates of their choice or volunteering to staff campaign functions. Many were newly energized by the "firsts" in the 2008 presidential campaign—Hillary Clinton as the first viable woman candidate to run for president, Barack Obama as the first viable African-American candidate to seek the White House, and Sarah Palin as the first woman to be chosen as a vice-presidential running mate on the Republican ticket.

Former NOW President Kim Gandy saw that phenomenon first-hand. As an active supporter and campaign-trail surrogate for Hillary Clinton, Gandy was amazed at the number of mothers she met who were motivated to get involved in the Clinton campaign mostly at the urging of their daughters—something she had not seen in prior campaigns.

"The idea of a woman president represented the fulfillment of concepts that these [mostly pre-teen and early teen] girls have been taught from childhood...that they could be anything and they were finally seeing this in a woman who was taking it to that level," said Gandy. Many of those mothers told her they were volunteering because their daughters were excited about the idea of a woman finally being president of the United States. Without the urging of their daughters, some of those mothers said they probably wouldn't have been involved in the campaign.

Gandy wasn't the only one to see the interest and excitement of school-aged children in the campaign process. *Washington Post* reporter and former *Time Magazine* correspondent Karen Tumulty also saw many campaign events filled with mothers and daughters, and says girls weren't the only ones focused on that historic presidential race. While Tumulty was covering John McCain's presidential campaign, she provided a sneak peek into that world for her own sons.

"They loved it! I had first taken my older son to New Hampshire in 2004, the weekend before the primary, when he was twelve. Two of my female editors did the same with their kids, and a few days after dragging them from event to event, we would marvel at how these four kids would sit at the breakfast table sounding like a miniature edition of The McLaughlin Group!" said Tumulty. Both of her sons went with her to New Hampshire in 2008, that time to get a taste of life on the campaign trail and the on-the-ground political process. "We were able to hitch a ride on

[McCain's] Straight Talk Express and when John McCain was done talking with reporters, he invited my kids back to chat with him one-on-one." As a result, she says, her kids became "McCain-iacs!" Tumulty offers a great piece of advice to parents: if you ever have a chance to take your child to a campaign event before there's too much Secret Service present, do it! She says it's an experience they'll never forget.

Fortunately, those kinds of experiences aren't reserved just for high-profile activists and national news reporters. We can all find opportunities to have our children see the political process up close with local events or fundraisers. Attorney and *MOMocrats* blog co-founder Glennia Campbell has frequently taken her son Alex with her to political events. Alex was a Hillary Clinton fan, even though Campbell and her husband supported other candidates during the 2008 presidential primary race. When they had a chance to see Clinton in person, Alex was so excited about the prospect of actually meeting her, Campbell and her husband agreed they should make it happen, even though it was after Clinton had dropped out of the race. "[Alex] pleaded, 'Take me! Take me! I want to tell Hillary what a good job she did,'" says Campbell.

And why had Alex chosen Hillary when his parents had made no secret of the fact that they had ultimately thrown their support to Barack Obama? "When I asked him why, he brought over a placemat we have with all the presidents on it, from Washington through Bush II. He put it in front of me and said, "See this? See any *girls* on this? I think Hillary should win because it's a *girl's* turn." When Alex finally met Clinton, Campbell says, "She looked genuinely pleased to see him and the other children at the event. She shook his hand and posed for pictures with him. Then he took her hand and told her, 'I really wanted you to be president. Thank you.' Her eyes softened, and she said, 'Thank you, too.'"

Photo courtesy Glennia Campbell

Sometimes parents just want their children to be present for certain politically historic moments, even if they don't get to meet the candidate of their choice in person. In her column "Domestic Disturbances," former *New York Times* columnist Judith Warner reported on a huge Sarah Palin rally in Northern Virginia two months before the 2008 election. She saw for herself the significance some mothers put on just being able to show their daughters that a Republican woman could have such a prominent role in national politics:

> I was...unable to find the press area in the crowd of about 15,000, [so] I was out with the "real" people. Which meant that I could hear everything from the podium and from the onlookers around me, but could see nothing, not, at least, until the mom beside me stopped struggling to balance atop her Little Tikes wagon with two toddlers in her arms and another screaming at her feet, and offered me a go at the view.

> 'It's *Sarah*. Sarah's going to be the vice president,' she had told the little girls, clad in their matching polka dot dresses. '*Sarah Palin.*'

In reading Warner's descriptions of the Palin rally's electric atmosphere and the excitement of the attendees, I wondered what Palin's fans loved more—Palin the person or Palin the idea, or what that idea could mean for their daughters. In the world of Republicans, Palin was the first woman to make it onto the highest national ticket. In 2008, the GOP had few women who were in visible positions of power and influence. For many Palin supporters, seeing a woman on stage who shared their ideas and ideals was motivating and empowering; for mothers, it was something important to be shared and experienced with their daughters.[79]

While there was a time when researchers disagreed about what kind of influence, if any, parents can have on the long-term political views of their children,[80] more recent research suggests that mothers are significant influencers in the political ideas and beliefs their children grow up with. A 2000 study by Oxygen Media and the Markle Foundation showed that in families where the mother is openly active in discussing politics, the children (especially girls) of those mothers are more interested in politics in the long term.[81] A study conducted after the 2008 presidential election found that mothers' roles played particular importance in their children's perceptions about the candidates, especially with regard to their families' views about Barack Obama's candidacy. For many voting mothers, the candidacies of Hillary Clinton and John McCain represented the status quo, whereas an Obama presidency offered change they wanted to see for their children's futures. These "Obama mamas," who became deeply involved in the political process, shared that experience with their children on many different levels, from watching speeches on TV together to stuffing envelopes to making their own political T-shirts.[82]

Teaching our children about politics doesn't have to come with the label "Democrat" or "Republican" on it. A broad historical education can help our kids find their own way to deciding what kind of political citizens they want to be. Former White House Press Secretary Dee Dee Myers says being immersed in the political world is just a fact of life in her household. Myers is a political analyst and her husband is a journalist, so it's difficult for her children to escape political discussion at home. But she and her husband have tried to incorporate history and current events in their dinner table discussions, rather than partisan politics, hoping that if their kids have a good grounding in historical context, they'll become engaged citizens. Having said that, Myers does fear the day they make their own decisions on the two things she feels most passionately about.[83]

"As a committed Democrat and Los Angeles Dodgers fan, I'm convinced that I'm going to visit one of my kids' dorm rooms in college, only to find Ronald Reagan and New York Yankees posters blanketing the walls!" she jokes.

Myers isn't the only high-profile parent who believes that the political education we give our children should be based on historical facts. On the heels of the 2008 presidential election, actor Richard Dreyfuss launched a project dedicated to grounding our children in the history of America, as well as what it really means to be a citizen, and teaching them the art of true political conversation rather than what passes as political dialogue on the cable news shouting head shows. [84]

There is a broad range of ways in which parents bring their children to political conversations. Although taking our children to vote with us is always a good start, that's just the beginning. Mothers across the country who refuse to describe themselves as "political" are increasingly sharing their stories online about the discussions they have with their children, the perspectives they bring to having political dialogues with their families, and the activities they share together on the road to political knowledge, participation, and critical thinking.

HE HAS A HIGHER SECURITY CLEARANCE THAN THE SCHOOL BUS DRIVER, SO SHOULDN'T YOU BE ABLE TO TRUST HIM WITH YOUR KIDS?
by Devra Renner, Parentopia blog

Being in the shadow of the nation's capital, one might think every public school within 50 miles of the beltway would be showing the speech President Obama delivered on the first day of school. A speech delivered in Arlington, Virginia. Can't get much more local than that. Well, think again.

Last week my son's elementary school principal sent home a note to all of the parents informing us that the president's speech to children will be shown in a couple of days. The note stated it was being sent home in response to several parental inquiries regarding the showing of President Obama's speech to school children in Arlington. It included information for parents who may wish to request an "opt out" for their child. The note shared that an alternate activity would be offered to those children who would not be watching the president's speech. I heard my grandmother's voice in my head: *"What has gotten into these people?"*

Indeed. Something is seriously amiss.

I remember in 1981 my mother was a delegate to the White House Conference on Aging. She brought me along with her and while she was spending her day caucusing and attending sessions, I was checking out the museums on the mall and coming back in time to meet her in the hotel ballroom for lunch and dinner. I even got to meet Ted Kennedy who hosted a reception for the New England delegation in his own office. He clapped me on the shoulder so hard I swore he must have thought I was choking on a carrot stick and said in a warm and booming voice, "Good to see you!" I also got to sit next to Christopher Dodd on the sofa and talk to him about how I was missing school to be in DC that week. He told me it was a really good reason and maybe I would be interested in working in DC one day. (Shut up. I can have a senator as my psychic friend.)

One afternoon during the conference I showed up for lunch and there was an airport-style metal detector set up outside of the door to the ballroom. I sauntered through it and made my way into the ballroom for lunch, oblivious to the man in the suit chasing me and yelling, *"Miss! You can't go in there!"* We didn't have the Secret Service routinely running around New Haven. I wasn't used to this sort of thing. So when I realized some big guy was running after me, I got scared and put my tush down in the first open chair I could find. It happened to be the table chock-full of delegates from Ohio.

When the Secret Service caught up to me at the table, I was instructed, *"Young lady, you will have to leave. The president will be speaking to the delegates and the delegates only. No guests. I am going to have to escort you out of the ballroom right now."* Next thing I knew, I hear voices of dissent saying things like, *"You are going to deny a child the opportunity to hear her president speak?"* and *"Sir, what you are doing is un-American. All Americans have the right to hear their president address his citizens,"* and finally, *"You stay right there dear, don't move. This man isn't taking you anywhere without a fight!"* Seeing that he was outnumbered, the agent made a hasty retreat. Advantage goes to the octogenarians from Ohio!

Was Ronald Reagan the candidate my family supported during the election? Oh hell no. However, he took the oath of office and became our nation's president. When my mother saw me sitting with my new Midwestern friends at lunch, she did not haul me out of the room telling me, *"Devra, we did not vote for this man, so you won't be hearing him. Here's five dollars, go get yourself a Happy Meal."* She waved to me and pointed to where she would be sitting so I could find her later.

And there I sat, listening to a president I did not agree with politically, yet I understood that because he took that oath of office to be *our* president, the Office of the President should be respected. I was taught by my parents to do that regardless of any political affiliation I might have personally. It wasn't all about me, it was all about protocol.

But it was the last line of President Reagan's speech which

gives insight into why the Ohio delegates went up against the Secret Service to secure my seat at the speech.

"We have much to offer, a great deal to offer. Let our children and our children's children one day say of us, the world that they live in is better because we were here before them."

My Ohio defenders were making sure I got my history lesson; the actions of those who came before me impact me now. Those who will come after me will be impacted by what I do at this present time.

Pithy lesson for a fourteen-year-old, but I still remember it over two decades later. And at the risk of sounding like I am writing a middle-school essay about the experience, I do believe that experience impacted me as a person as well as a parent. (Although this realization came much later). In 1981, I was merely a rebellious teen who, in my mind, was making fun of the president's shellacked hair and was blown away that a group of "old folks" were even more badass than I was.

So why on earth an "opt-out" now for children to hear the president speak? What lesson does it teach our children? If we don't agree with a person we pretend that person doesn't exist. How disrespectful. This is the President of the United States of America. Why do we give the Sally Foster fundraising presentation more respect than the POTUS? I haven't been sent home an "opt-out" for that craptastic waste of time held during school hours.

I suppose it could be argued parental involvement in education means parents should be able to preview the president's speech before it is shown to our children. OK, but are parents reviewing every textbook and lesson plan the teacher is presenting to our children? Are we requiring invited guests for a school-wide assembly meet with concerned parents prior to performing or presenting to the student body? How about we don't let our kids check out school library books before we read the volumes ourselves? Do you have time for any of that? What if it were required of parents that we do all of that for every child we sent to school? Ridiculous, right?

Sadly we are living in a society where ridiculous currently rules. Kanye West at the Video Music Awards? Ridiculous. Serena Williams at the U.S. Open? Ridiculous. Congressman Joe Wilson on the

Congressional floor shouting 'You lie!' at the president? Ridiculous.

Again I hear my grandmother's voice asking: *"What's gotten into these people?"* We all know that question is meant as a rhetorical way to bring attention to a problem someone sees but may not be able to do anything about personally.

How about we change what we hear just a little? Ask a question in our own minds so the answer to it holds us personally accountable for our decisions and our actions? After all, parents are the primary role models for our children. It's important we be able to identify if we are, in fact, being ridiculous. Surely there is a question we can propose as a candidate to keep our own choices in check.

I nominate, *"What's gotten into me?"* Got another you want to nominate? I'll be happy to listen to whatever you have to say— regardless of whether I agree with it or not.

MY CHILDREN GIVE ME HOPE FOR THE FUTURE
by Sarah Braesch, Sarah and the Goon Squad blog

This morning my daughter Claudia and I were talking about voting. I explained to her that if you were over 18 and a United States citizen you got to pick who you wanted to be your leader. I tried to simplify it (I don't even think I could explain the electoral college if I wanted to) and I told her that whoever got the most votes would win.

To illustrate this point I did what any good mommy blogger would do—I Googled a picture of Barack Obama and John McCain.

I pointed at each man and said this is Barack Obama and this is John McCain. Then we looked at a different picture of them and I pointed them out again. Then we looked at another.

I asked Claudia if she could tell which one was which.

She pointed at the man on the left. "This is Narack Ofama," (meh, close enough for a four-year-old) "and this is John McCain.

You know how I can tell?"

I asked her how.

"They have different color hair."

While I sit here and worry that there are Americans out there who won't vote for a good man just because of the color of his skin, I can be assured that at least one of the next generation of voters didn't even notice the difference.

That gives me hope.

THIS WHOLE CAMPAIGN LOOKS A LOT DIFFERENT TO AN EIGHT-YEAR-OLD
by Joanne Bamberger, PunditMom blog

Trying to explain our electoral process to an eight-year-old is like trying to help your child make sense of why the boys who like you in the classroom pick on you during recess.

It's all a bit inscrutable.

What's even harder is trying to help a second-grader grasp that while the election coverage that mommy is addicted to has been going on since before she started this school year, that things won't be over until she's settled into next year's school routine.

"But **WHY?**" is PunditGirl's continual response when I try to explain why we don't have a new President yet. We had this discussion after the New Hampshire primary:

PunditGirl: "But who won last night?"

PunditMom: "Well, Hillary Clinton for the Democrats and John McCain for the Republicans."

PG: "So which one is president?"

PM: "Well, no one yet because all the other states have to vote first, then we all vote again."

PG (with eight-year-old scowl): Well…then who's ahead? Who has the most points?"

PM: "It doesn't work like that. First, we have to see who gets the most points for each side, then those two candidates get to talk some more, through the summer, about who they think would do a better job and then we get to vote again, but not until November."

PG (with visible shock and disgust): "You mean we won't know who has the most points until after I'm in *third grade*?"

Kind of puts the ridiculously long election season in perspective, doesn't it?

When I told PunditGirl that Mommy's first choice, John Edwards, had dropped out of the race, she was horrified. Even though PunditGirl is supporting Hillary (her theory being that if you're a girl, you should vote for the girl!), she was pretty exasperated at the idea of a candidate giving up. The idea of a candidate dropping out of the presidential race is a ludicrous one for my budding pundit. In her mind, if you get in you stay in until someone wins.

PG: "But Mom, he can't know the future! What if all of a sudden more people start to vote for him? Then won't he be sorry?"

Sort of like when you're playing *Sorry!*—you never know who's going to win, because fortunes can turn on a dime.

Ah, young optimism! I need to get me some of that!

PURCHASING POWER OF WOMEN
by Ilina Ewen, Dirt & Noise blog

I have been having some heavy conversations with my sons lately. Racism. Race relations. Sexism. Gender equality. Heavy stuff for any age, but even more so with a five- and a three-year-old. Admittedly not the typical fare for carpool lines and kitchen conversations everywhere. But my sons sit perched at the breakfast bar while I cook dinner and we talk. Mostly they ask questions, and I wrack my brain coming up with honest yet meaningful answers that will make sense to their innocent blank slates. I tread lightly, knowing this will likely be the beginning of their developing self-awareness. So what's the catalyst for such heady talk at our house?

Barack Obama.

You see, my children are mixed-race, first-generation Americans. My husband is a born and bred Midwesterner from a town of five hundred people. I am an Indian girl who was born in Calcutta, a city of 16 million. I say it's kismet that brought us together 31 years after our births.

My sons are starting to recognize that we look different from each other, and that I look different from other moms. The beauty of childhood is that they view these differences with no judgment, no preconception, no expectations, and no bigotry. Some call it naiveté. I call it bliss.

I spent the better part of 2008 campaigning for Barack Obama in my home state of North Carolina. Political chatter surrounded us, and we tuned in the children when we felt it was appropriate. Sometimes they were walking Obama billboards sporting their "*Yes We Can*" T-shirts.

On Election Day of 2008, I showed a picture of the past 43 presidents to my sons and asked what they noticed about the people. First they said, "There are no girls, Mommy." Home run! Then my son "Bird" said, "They all look like Daddy. They are pink." I explained that the terms we use are white, and black or African American, to which he animatedly replied, "But we are brown, Mommy. And no one is white. They are pink!" How could I argue with such logic?

But after Obama's election, our family conversation turned from how we talk about skin color in our country to how women are often treated differently from men. That didn't sit well with my sons, either.

I happened to flip on the TV during Obama's press conference about signing the Lilly Ledbetter Fair Pay Act. The boys shouted for me to move so they too could see the television. Obama! Obama! We all sat mesmerized as he spoke, with a tenacious and victorious Ledbetter at his side. That moment was important for our family, not just because it was the new president's first official bill signing. I explained that when Mommy and Daddy met, we both had the exact same jobs, but Daddy got paid more money than I did. I told them that I had actually been in the job longer, but Daddy earned more money. "No fair!" they shouted in unison. I regaled them with the tale about me marching into our manager's office demanding an explanation…and a raise. My next pay stub reflected a significant bump in pay that equaled my husband's. Whether it was my gumption or my boss's fear I'll never know. I explained to my sons how many, many women earn less money than men doing the same things. I told them that that lady standing next to Obama got fed up, and

America finally listened.

It's no secret that women, while not occupying the driver's seat or C-Suite in most cases, still control the nation's purse strings. Women influence where, how, and when dollars are spent. We are the ones in our families who often dictate most major purchase decisions. That power is exponentially boosted when those women are mothers. I'm venturing to guess the same holds true in euros, pounds, and rupees, too. We make the decisions about tuition, hockey gear, life insurance, stock picks, vacations, braces and how to create our business start-ups.

You get the idea.

But companies haven't figured that out yet. It's a shame that so many businesses still talk down to women like we're a bunch of ninnies who don't want to ruin our manicures and coiffed hairdos. It's a shame that there are still some among us who continue to think we are pantyhose-wearing, bon bon-eating girls who have to ask our husbands or daddies for an allowance.

As the mother of boys, I hope to raise them in a manner that debunks gender biases. My three-year-old's favorite color is pink. My five-year-old loves to draw and paint. My husband often cooks spectacular dinners, and he has breakfast duty on weekends, for which he spoils us with crème brulée French toast and the like. We share duties as primary care givers. And we both contribute to our family's bottom line. My goal is to raise my sons as open-minded citizens who see the worth in all people, regardless of race, gender, or anything else that adults deem worthy of judgment. And I hope, as their mother, that the world grants them the same respect.

OUR DAUGHTERS ARE PAYING ATTENTION
by Joanne Bamberger, PunditMom blog

Stern. Witchy. The 'b' word that rhymes with witchy. Shrill. Scolding.

I suspect that few of us would allow our husbands to use those words to describe us (even if they think them on occasion) when they are in front of our children, and especially not in the presence of our daughters.

Yet, innumerable journalists, especially men, have found it perfectly acceptable to describe Hillary Clinton in those words plus many others that get used to describe powerful and assertive women, as she runs for president. They are hateful and prejudicial phrases that convey an underlying meanness and insecurity about females who challenge traditional stereotypes about women in our society.

If these men, many of whom undoubtedly have daughters, paid the tiniest bit of attention to what their children are focused on, they might rethink the vocabulary they are using to pillory Hillary.

Because believe it or not, our kids are paying attention. Even our youngest children.

Exhibit A? I volunteered for lunch table duty at my daughter's school one week during the campaign, and I was shocked that the conversation topic of choice at two tables full of first- and second-graders was the presidential election.

Kids were polling each other about whether they wanted to vote for Barack or Hillary (sorry, I did not hear any child say they were for John McCain, but I think that's just the neighborhood we live in). I didn't catch the reason that the boys wanted Obama to be president but the girls were clear—Hillary should be president because it's time for a girl to have a turn.

Eight-year-old logic at its finest.

But if seven- and eight-year-olds are choosing to talk about this on their own—really, I swear, I did NOT plant that seed at the lunch table—then you know they're also paying attention to the words we and news commentators choose to describe the candidates.

At the time, *Cleveland Plain Dealer* columnist Connie Schultz wrote, "We bruise our daughters when we bash Hillary Clinton." She was generally talking about girls a bit older than the ones I sat with last week who were scarfing down chicken nuggets and jelly sandwiches, but the point is the same—our daughters are focused and invested in this presidential race because "a girl"—someone like them—wants to be in charge and make decisions.

Girl power is a very big thing for elementary school girls.

Since that's the case, we all need to be careful how we describe

Hillary, because you can be sure that whatever we call Senator Clinton, our daughters are going to find a way to internalize that.

My second-grade daughter, like so many, thinks she can make good decisions and could possibly be president one day. But if we allow journalists, men or women, to continue to bash Hillary and her historic effort, we may as well tell our girls there's no point to having that dream, or any dream, because they'll only be mocked and ridiculed just the way Hillary Clinton has been.

YOU SAY YOU WANT A REVOLUTION
by Linda Lowen, About.com Women's Issues blog

Barack Obama may have offered change we need. But my two daughters would have missed out on a certain revolution had it not been for Hillary Clinton. And in doing so, they might never have discovered the strength that comes from the conviction of their beliefs.

Jaye at 16 was a veteran of local theatre and preferred Broadway show tunes. But thirteen-year-old Em lived and breathed rock. When she found out that Projekt Revolution—an annual tour featuring cutting-edge bands—was coming to town, she just had to be there.

"You're thirteen!" I spluttered. "I'll be turning fourteen in three weeks!" she argued. "This could be my birthday present."

"Who're you going to go with? I'm not taking you," I grumbled.

"Jaye will go with me. I know she'll wanna go," Em insisted. (For the social aspects, yes. The music? Not so much.)

"I'm not letting you two go to the concert alone; it's miles away and what would you do if something happened?" I knew this standard mom defense would be the clincher.

"Mom, you'll be within walking distance! It's on the same day you're working the Hillary Clinton booth!"

She had me at Hillary.

Weeks earlier, an item in my local paper asked for volunteers to staff Senator Hillary Clinton's presidential campaign booth during the annual state fair. As a long-time supporter, I had committed to an all-day shift from 10 a.m. to 10 p.m.

Conveniently, the concert would start at noon and wrap up

shortly after I was done. I'd be less than an eighth of a mile away the whole time. Is it any wonder both my daughters ended up as Hillary supporters?

I'm telling this story because by Election Day, both Jaye (now 17) and Em (now 15) had endured a crushing amount of peer pressure that would have broken the average teen.

Not to drink, do drugs, or have sex. But to support Barack Obama.

At home, our bookshelves were lined with *The Case for Hillary Clinton* by Susan Estrich, *Hillary's Choice* by Gail Sheehy, *The Girls on the Van: Covering Hillary* by Beth Harpaz, and other pro-Hillary titles. At school, Obama owned the hearts and minds of all their non-Republican classmates.

Strong women raise strong daughters. Thus Jaye didn't keep her mouth shut as most teenage girls do. She argued why Hillary would be a better choice as the Democratic nominee. But at every turn, she was shouted down. Friends grew angry at her and told her to shut up.

Eventhough her crowd is a smart, creative, liberal-minded mix of straight and gay, black and white, Jaye heard several slander Hillary and mock women as leaders. Inculcated against sexism at an early age, Jaye has always been aware of gendered language; comments that fly under others' radar rankle her.

The situation got so bad that she came home one day with red eyes. "Mom, they hate it when I say anything good about Hillary. But if I ask them to tell me why they support Obama, or name some issues they agree with, nobody says a word. They just want to vote for him because it's cool."

Kids, teens, young adults form their own opinions of political events and candidates. That's a good thing. But how they inform themselves worries me. Following the crowd just because "everybody does it" diminishes the intent of our forefathers, who broke away from the status quo, took a risk, and formed a more perfect union. It negates the sacrifices of our foremothers, who were beaten, jailed, force-fed, and humiliated so we could gain the right to vote and exercise it down the road in support of a woman candidate.

I realize my daughters won't be political carbon-copies of me.

I'm staunchly pro-choice, while Em opposes abortion because it ends human life. (I respect her conviction and hope it's never personally put to the test.)

I also respect that my daughters are sophisticated enough to recognize a wolf in sheep's clothing. When Sarah Palin came on the scene, they were as suspicious of the thin "pro-women" veneer stretched over her campaign as I was. They didn't regard Bristol Palin's pregnancy as anything other than unfortunate, asking "Why wouldn't she use birth control if she were going to have sex? That's just stupid."

When I thought about traveling out of state for a few days to help with Clinton's ground campaign (and Obama's too, later on), they both said, "Mom, just do it. We'll manage fine without you. You can really make a difference if you volunteer."

For some families, religion is like politics. Out of a misplaced sense of politeness, you don't speak about it at work, school, or social gatherings; and you only pay attention to it once a week on Sundays, or once a year around Election Day. In our family, every dinner table discussion is a religious and political open-mic night. We argue about God and faith (Em still doesn't believe God exists), politics, and women's issues. We don't always agree, but it helps me to understand how my daughters' political opinions are shaped, and how peer pressure plays a part.

Maybe this approach has made my daughters too bold for most guys' tastes. Neither has had a boyfriend in high school. But that puts them in the same boat as Hillary Rodham. She didn't meet Bill until Yale Law School. When I compare her youth to that of Sarah Heath Palin, who eloped with her high school sweetheart and had a baby eight months later, I know which path I'd rather choose for my daughters.

But again, that's not my choice. That's theirs.

I don't spend too much time worrying, though. By standing up for Hillary, they also stood up for themselves and by extension, every other girl who was ever told "no" and still continued to work toward "yes." By supporting the loser instead of "going along" (as women have always done) and backing the winner, they filled me with maternal pride, renewed conviction that the good fight is worth it, and feminist glee that in a choice between change and revolution, as long as they hold steadfast to what they believe in, they know it's gonna be all right.

BEST FRIENDS ACROSS POLITICAL PARTIES
by Diana Prichard, Diana Prichard blog

My daughter has the makings of a Democrat. Her best friend, a Republican.

They're only seven, but the *real* politicians could learn a thing or two from their ability to engage in respectful, rational discourse and continue friendship and a working relationship across "party divides."

This past Saturday we made an almost five-hour trek into Chicago to visit the evils that are the American Girl Place. Three floors of complete chaos. Our girls live in the country, the closest town to us has a population of 300. There are no homeless here. And if there are, they certainly aren't camped out on the one short block of downtown sidewalk available with a cardboard sign looking for handouts.

Naturally during the close to six miles we walked that day we passed quite a few homeless men and a couple of women with signs. I noticed The Princess's eyes lingering on them from the very first person we saw. I could feel through her hand, her steps slowing just slightly as we passed, everything I'd ever told her about some people not having homes or clothes or toys so she must remain grateful coming to life. In her face I could almost see the revelation. *Mom did not make this up, those people don't have a home or clothes or toys. Oh. My. Gawd.*

I'm not sure if she needed time to let it all gel in her mind or if she was simply too distracted by *everything* there was to see, but she did not say anything about the homeless she so clearly noticed until we had already boarded the train and begun our trip home that night.

"Mom?" She paused after my name just long enough to catch my glance from the seat beside her. "Did you see those people? With the signs?"

"Which ones, honey?"

"You know, the ones sitting by the buildings..."

"Yes, I saw them. What did they make you think?"

"They were hungry, I think."

"Ahh, what makes you think that?"

"Their signs, they said that they needed help because they were very hungry."

I was about to ask her what she thought about it all when her friend jumped in from across the aisle.

"Yeah, but they'll probably just take it and buy junk."

Here the look on The Princess's face was one of pure exasperation. "They're HUNGRY. They need to EAT!"

Her friend shot back nonchalantly. "Well, I think they'll just probably buy junk like necklaces and pearls and then try to sell them for more money for *more* junk! Not food. That's why I don't like them out there."

I interjected just for a moment to keep them on track; they are seven after all, and if they were going to have this discussion they might as well take something from it other than the realization that there are different opinions on the topic of homelessness. "Girls, you both make good points. Some of them probably really are hungry, and others might really be tricking us with those signs to try to get money to spend on things they don't need." I figured for now necklaces and pearls were preferable to them knowing the *real* things often bought that are not needed. Things like crack, vodka and Xanax to help them deal with seven-year-old girls who are already on to their game, for instance. "Do you have any ideas about how you might be able to tell the difference? How do we deal with them if we can't tell who is telling us the truth?"

They thought about just asking them, but if they'd lied on the sign, chances are they'd lie to your face as well. And then there's the problem of there being so many of them: how do you have time to stop and talk to them all? They thought about not helping any of them, because there's no way to know which are being truthful; they weren't sure it was fair to write everyone off across the board. They thought about helping all, but weren't sure the very small allowance they work very hard to earn would go far. They didn't come to a resolution, but they worked together as they tried, and they both went away with a broader perspective of the situation.

As it turns out political, moral dilemmas are essentially identical whether you're seven or 70. Time, limited resources, and the desire to help but not be taken advantage of all prevail. The only difference? Seven-year-olds are much more capable of not taking the other party's position personally, and so they work together to find a resolution. Even if they're not immediately successful at least they can say they tried, together.

Politicians take note.

TEARS IN MY SALAD
by Kim Moldofsky, Scrambled Cake blog

My eyes welled up as I stood chopping veggies, but no onions were in sight. I was near tears because I was listening to a story on National Public Radio about a camp for children whose parents died in the Iraq War. The piece was more than gut-wrenching. It was a call to action. I can no longer sit and listen to these stories. I must do something to help end the war.

Months ago I asked my boys what we can do to stop the war. *Us? Our family? Don't you mean what can the president do?*

I explained that in a democracy, it's up to the people to tell the President what to do. Not the other way around (in theory, at least). But we never acted on our discussion. Not until last week when I got invited to a war vigil. So I gathered up poster board and markers and set the boys loose. Well, sort of. First my boys and their friend started printing colorful messages like "Bring the Soldiers Home" and "Soldiers Come Home." Seven year-old Pikachu's created a more abstract message of peace with flags and countries and tears and...

And then the boys began asking thoughtful, probing questions, *Who's fighting with us and who are the enemies? How many people have died?*

Finally, as happens in our house, things degraded. Rapidly.
Can I draw fighting? No.
Can I draw guns shooting? No.

Can I draw just guns? No! This is a peace vigil for goodness sake!

I already drew a soldier, is it okay if he has a gun? Soldiers have guns, you know. Ugh. Always a loophole. Fine, the soldier can have the gun, but after you draw it I'm putting away the markers!

The vigil (or war protest, as the boys liked to call it) attracted about 40 or so like-minded people, including four families with children to a busy intersection to spread a message of peace. Many who drove past our group honked or waved "peace fingers" in support. Okay, one guy waved a different finger and shouted something that I couldn't quite make out, except for the words m-----f-----. But overall the people driving through town were cool with our message.

Image with permission by Kim Moldofsky

"I didn't know standing around with a sign was going to be so fun," said Smartypants at the end of the muggy evening. We both felt like we'd done something good, something worthwhile. (Pikachu, not so much; he's rather hawkish.)

I can't say if I'm entering a new era of political involvement, but I did just invite Senator Obama and his wife to meet me and a crew of my mommy blogging friends. Now what will I serve them if they show up?

RAISING A CITIZEN
by Veronica Arreola, Viva la Feminista blog

My husband and I like to joke that we are raising a candidate.

We are both fans of the Kennedy clan, as most Mexicans are. We both grew up in families that talked fondly of all the Kennedy brothers, and my great-grandmother had a portrait of JFK next to The Last Supper. The Kennedys were our fairytale. We didn't dream of being rescued into good fortune; we were raised to believe we could make it happen. We are also quite aware of how the lore of how Joe

Kennedy raised the boys to be public officials, they were groomed and they served this country. This is where our daughter comes in.

First she was named after Elizabeth Cady Stanton. I went through every baby name book along with a list of my favorite feminists in history. Stanton was a suffragist who wrote like a machine while raising seven children, and her collaboration with Susan B. Anthony is often overlooked in history books. We also liked that Elizabeth could be shortened to Buffy, our beloved vampire slayer, or to a plethora of other nicknames. I also kept in mind a friend who said that our daughters should have names that sound authoritative when said after "Judge" or "Senator." OK, so Buffy would be saved for the dinner table.

Her education started early and it began with our selection of children's books. One of her first board books was about Martin Luther King Jr.; one on Coretta followed a few years later when I finally found it. I surrounded her with books about women in history, including one on her namesake and one on campaigning. But it wasn't just a book education I sought for her. Oh no. I took her out to door knock for a congressional candidate. She loved it. What almost three-year-old could resist taking a walk on a sunny day handing out stickers and signs to people? Honestly, she loved handing people information.

Later in the year I became a precinct captain for an aldermanic candidate. I walked our precinct as often as I could and yes, my daughter asked to come along. I know that at three-and-a-half, she was asking to spend time with me, but the point is that I allowed her to do just that. I don't want to indoctrinate my daughter with my politics or beliefs; rather I want to show her how I live my life, why I make the decisions I do and what I do from my office, as well as what I do to participate in our community. I have this cute photo of her mimicking me on the phone reading from the script. She heard me say it so many times at the campaign office and at home that she was able to repeat most of it. She soon thought that we were campaigning for a woman named Naisy Dolar Dot Com. Naisy ran a great campaign, and I truly believe that because she was the mom of two young children (her oldest was the same age as my daughter) that the office was kid-friendly. That made a huge difference in the amount of time I was able to work for her. More importantly it gave my daughter a sense of belonging and place. She never was made to feel like she was a nuisance, except when I shushed her during meetings.

Her dad and I talk to her about politicians we see on TV or in magazines. One day we were in waiting for my eye doctor and I pointed to the cover of *Time Magazine* and said, "That's our next president." I was only half joking, but more seriously explained that the smiling man was Senator Barack Obama, our senator. We chatted about why Mommy liked him, why she didn't and what a senator was.

In June 2007, *Brain, Child* magazine asked on its blog if parents should raise their children with their political views. I responded with a simple, "Of course." A commenter went off about people like me teaching hate—"You don't think your kids see your hatred and anger toward this country?"

Hatred? Really? Any hatred I have is about how our country was, and in some cases still is, being run and it's more frustration than hatred, even if I do swear about the government a lot. Rather than teaching hatred for this country, I teach my daughter about respect. Respect for us, her teachers, family, and friends. We also try—it's hard—to model respect for different tastes and views. Throughout the 2008 primary season, we talked to her about who was running and why we were voting the way we did. We took her with us to vote, not just this time, but every time we vote. Our neighbor, who is akin to her godmother, took her to vote for Obama in the general election as we decided to vote early due to the threat of super-long lines. But never once during discussing issues and candidates with her, despite our loathing, did we disparage Bush. She asked if he could be president again. I simply explained to her that in January Bush's turn was over and kept my "Thank Gawd!" in my head.

But hate? Never. I don't even like to say I hate pickles in front of her—and I really hate pickles. To her, I really, really, really don't like them. Love is what we talk about. We extend our love far outside our blood family. We celebrate holidays with friends and members of our chosen family. I take my daughter to organizing events and meetings to show her how much love goes into the work I do. She has been to anti-war and equal-marriage rallies and it is explained to her in terms of simple love and respect.

Which is why I can't understand how people who believe in forbidding two loving people to marry, in racism (not just blatant, but subtle/institutional), and that their religion is better than any other, can even suggest that progressives or feminists preach hate or brainwash our children. If teaching my daughter to respect and love all who share our planet is brainwashing, then I am guilty. If teaching her that those who don't are still to be respected (I'm still working on this one!) is hateful, then I am guilty.

Instilling values in children is what parents do. That is your intention and my intention from the start. If we let them make all their own decisions, they would be lost. I don't tell her, unlike a dear friend of mine, that supporters of a certain U.S. congressman don't get candy while at a parade. But I did tell her I liked Senator Obama because we both "like the same things."

I view a lot of what I do in life through a feminist lens. It's not easy, but it's not cheesy either. I don't vote just because I have something to say or want someone to do something for me, but I know the history of women's suffrage and well, I am so not going to tempt the ghost of Alice Paul.

I will teach our daughter that history, as well as the sad facts like the disenfranchisement of ex-felons and the changes at the Chicago Housing Authority, destroyed the only "poor people's" voting bloc this city knew, and that despite our huffing over democracy, money can still buy an election. But I will also certainly stress that many women fought long and hard for her to have the right to vote, that it is not something to take for granted, and certainly that she can't complain about this or that if she opts out of voting.

When I think about the awesome fact that she has an opinion on whether we should have voted for Barack or Hillary (she wanted a tie, she likes them both) AND that she is willing to voice this opinion, I have to be super proud of her. And honestly, I'm pretty proud of us as parents that we instilled that sense of entitlement in her.

Will she ever run for office? I haven't a clue. But I know that she will grow up knowing that she should always vote and that the first presidential race that she may remember had a woman, a Latino and a black man in the mix.

We're not raising a candidate, we're raising a citizen.

(NOT) PASSING ON WHAT MATTERS TO US MOST
by Jen Lemen, PBS Supersisters blog

I recently found myself in a crisis in the back of a Land Rover in rural Tanzania.

We were on a tour of the poorest of the poor—a gentle-hearted group of families suffering from malnutrition and abject poverty in a tiny drought-afflicted village. This was one of those heart-stopping moments that stay with you forever—and none of it was registering with my kids. One was reading a comic book and the other was 200 pages into a vampire book. Neither looked up when we pulled up or when we we wheleft. They had something else to do. They were tired. They were bored.

I wasn't sure whether to pull the old mom card—you know, the hissing command issued in the ear that says get it together now—*or else*. I didn't know if I should just let them be because the situation was so intense (even for someone 30 years their senior) or launch into some self-righteous speech. In the end, I decided on something in between: a firm request to put the books down and pay attention—at least while we were on the tour.

In the end, I'm not sure if any of it made a difference.

I know it's probably naive to expect more from kids, but I was really affected by their apparent lack of interest. "I don't know what to say," one child explained later in the day without an ounce of guilt or concern. "I have my hands full with my own life. I don't have that much space to think about helping someone else."

I still haven't completely recovered from that statement. It leaves me without any words at all.

Reflecting on it now two weeks after the fact, I can see that my concern is centered around values—that set of guidelines or principles that we've chosen to give our lives direction and meaning. How is it that my kids in that instance so quickly passed over something that fully engaged my values? How is it that an experience that was rife with opportunity for a response and the most simple, kind reaction seemed to strike them as no big deal? And maybe this is the most important question of all: how can we know if our children are internalizing *at all* our most essential values?

After this trip, I have no idea.

I want my kids to understand they have choices. And I want them to feel connected to a personal sense of power as well as to the consequences their choices generate. But what happens when that understanding of power, choices, and consequences leaves out caring? What happens when kids decide being compassionate is optional? Do you pass it off as just a phase? Or is it time to march everyone to Habitat for Humanity every weekend for the rest of their childhood?

I'm still asking myself these questions.

What matters to you when you think about who your children might become? What values do you hope they decide to carry with them into the future? What do **you** do when it looks like they're missing what you'd hoped was an obvious invitation to what matters to you most?

(Reprinted from pbsparents.org with permission of the Public Broadcasting Service)

THE LEANING TOWER OF POLITICS
by Tanis Miller, Attack of the Redneck Mommy blog

Growing up, my parents stressed the importance of voting and exercising your civic duty upon my impressionable mind. They made a big deal of elections and when I finally turned 18 and could cast my first ballot, they drove me to the voting station and proudly watched as I marked my very first X. I don't remember who I voted for, but I remember thinking that it was my very first adult responsibility and I was proud of myself for participating in our democratic elections.

My party lost. But that didn't matter to me; all that mattered was the fact I voted. My voice was heard. It may have helped if I hadn't voted for the Marijuana Party, but hey, I was 18.

After my parents had voted , I remember asking them whom

they had voted for. They refused to tell me because they didn't want to influence my ideologies and they wanted me to make my own informed decision without any influence from them.

It didn't matter how much I wheedled and needled them, they weren't going to spill the beans. To this day, I still have no idea who they support, but I'm fairly confident it isn't the dope smokers. Just a hunch.

I'm now a bit of an election hound. I love politics. Not enough to consider tossing my hat into the ring, but enough to soak up every bit of election trivia I can get my mitts on and suck it up like a sponge. I only wish Canadian politics was half as feisty as those Yankee elections.

But we Canucks are a quieter breed. We're still a dirty people; we just tend to keep it in the bedroom and out of the elections. Sooo boring. Mind you, after taking a look at our past and current leaders, I can only offer a prayer of thanks. I really don't want to be imagining any of them getting busy on a blue dress. Ew.

Unlike my parents, there is much screaming-and-yelling civil debate about politics in our home. Boo has a wildly different political ideology than I do. If it were up to him, the world would all be doing a stiff-legged march with a pert salute, as all bowed to his iron will. If it were left to me, well, let's just say we'd all be seeing rainbows and unicorns and having a good time. Wink, wink.

Because Boo and I have such vastly different political leanings, it has never troubled me to talk politics in front of our children. As we shout at each other or politely discuss one party's platform versus another, our children get to hear both sides of the spectrum and form their own opinions.

I can't help it if they grow up and choose my ideology because they love me more, and I am more articulate with my thoughts and better prepared to debate. *Heh heh.*

Recently, the beautiful and bountiful province of Alberta underwent the electoral process to elect the government. I kept waiting for things to heat up like the American primaries that I avidly follow and drool over, but it was nothing but a snooze fest. Yawn.

Still, it goes against every fiber of my being to be apathetic, and

I mustered up the bare minimum of interest. Come Election Day, I picked my kids up at lunchtime and hauled them off to the polling station with me. I think it is important that they see the democratic process in action.

I mean, all those middle-aged women volunteering to man the polls are truly exciting. Are they going to knit or will they be reading a book? Will it be a romance smut novel or a bloodthirsty mystery? Talk about the height of excitement.

After staring at a row of rural maps and trying to figure out just where the fack I live and what polling station to vote at, I gathered the troops up and marched over to cast my ballot. Fric and Frac were excited to be included in the process. (Read: I promised to buy them an ice cream if they didn't act like Satan's Spawn for 15 minutes and didn't induce any heart palpitations in the elderly.)

As I went to mark my X for the candidate of choice, I briefly explained to the kids who each person was and what their party stood for. Of course, I remained neutral and diplomatic. I would never try to shove my own personal leftist spin down their throats. *Heh, heh*. They were about as interested in my highly educational speech as they are in putting their laundry away. Still, they kept their mouths shut and pretended like I wasn't sucking their brain matter out their noses with a straw.

The lure of ice cream at lunch hour on a school day is a powerful incentive.

I had to threaten them to be quiet about my left leanings inside the polling station as I was surrounded by a pack of gun-toting conservatives who would think nothing of tarring and feathering me before burning me on the altar of their Ann Coulter-loving ways.

I'm blonde. I'm not stupid.

As I drove them back to school, they happily licked and slurped their cones as I droned on and on about why it is so important to vote in an election. Even if the election is as terminally boring as this one was.

"People died defending our freedom and right to choose our leaders," I said.

Slurp, slurp.

"You can't complain if you don't vote," I continued.

Lick, lick.

"The world will come to a screeching halt if I ever discover either of you were too damned lazy to get off your skinny little arses and cast a ballot. Hot pokers in the belly button will be nothing next to the wrath of your politically crazy mother if she ever finds out you morphed into an apathetic, mindless twit who doesn't have the sense God gave a gopher. Got that?" I promised.

They momentarily looked up from their cones and gave me the holy-shit-our-mother-is-bat-shit-crazy look and then promised to always vote as they resumed their ministrations at hand.

As I was shoving them out of my car to send them back to the land of teeny boppers and mean girls, Frac turned around and asked me whom I voted for.

"It doesn't matter who I voted for Frac. It just matters that I voted," I emphasized. "Now get to class."

"Come on Frac, let's go." Fric tugged at her brother. I felt a moment of parental pride as I watched the two of them trudge off together. They're growing up so fast.

Then I heard Fric turn to her brother and tell him, "She voted for the same party she always does. The losers. Just check to see who came in last place and you'll know who Mom voted for."

Damn. She's smart, I thought as I rolled up the window.

"When I grow up, I'm voting like Dad. He only votes for the winners," Fric told her brother. My jaw dropped as I watched them high-five one another and giggle as they walked through the school doors.

Apparently, my work is NOT done here. I must get better at either selling my ideology to them or resign myself to the fact I am raising not one, but two, Alex P. Keatons.

Heaven help me.

DEAR OHIO DEMOCRATIC PARTY
by Dawn Friedman, This Woman's Work blog

Dear Ohio Democratic Party,

Listen, I know your volunteers are young. I know most of them are college students because I used to volunteer when I was a college student, and I remember looking around the table and seeing a lot of other passionate young folks with occasional retirees. What I didn't see much of at those volunteer trainings were people my age—middle-aged-ish. You know, people with jobs and kids.

And so I understand that your phone-bank workers don't get me and that when they call me to volunteer they are unlikely to appreciate the reality of my life, even when I tell it to them. So they may not believe me when I say, "I am extremely busy because I have two home-schooled children and freelance work and volunteer work for another outfit—BUT if you have any one-off jobs I can do with my kids, I can do them. Because I'd be happy to give my kids a chance to be involved, and I would like to help."

So this means no data entry. Like I said, I want to do something WITH my kids, and I'm pretty sure that the young man on the phone has never tried to do data entry with kids running around like small lunatics or he wouldn't suggest it.

See, having kids makes things harder. It doesn't mean we don't care (so please, could you put away your heavy sighs and guilt-attempting annoyance?), it means we are freaking busy. You want parents—especially working parents—to help you get out the vote? Find a way to involve us with our kids. Let me tell you, a lot of families would love to have their kids lend a hand. Why not have a family night envelope-stuffing party? I remember doing this for some Oregon Women's Fund organization way back when I lived in Portland—they got us pizzas and we stuffed the hell out of their capital campaign envelopes. Kids over a certain age could totally do that, and many of them are more than happy to work for pizza. This is your chance to grow your future activists! Teach them about the political process and give their parents a chance to be involved! Because I can do data entry if you can find something for my kids to do while I do it.

Unfortunately, even though I had time to come up with this great pizza-party idea and the time to type it here, I don't have time to organize it. But you, dearest college student likely without a job with the adorable apologetic and awkward phone manner who called me last night, you do. I know this because I had time when I was a college student even when I was working full time. Because you know what is a bigger time suck than exam week? Every dang week with kids. I am not even kidding. You can't believe it now, but I am telling you that it is true. So don't ask whether I'm sure I can't do this or that. Don't offer me jobs I can't do with my kids when I told you that my kids are part of my volunteer deal—come up with something! Talk to your supervisor! Say, "There is this untapped source of energy and it is called PARENTS WITH CHILDREN!"

Otherwise, sure, keep me on your list. Call me closer to the election. Like I said, I'll hang door signs because I can bring my kids, but you can keep that data entry to your own self.

CHAPTER THREE

More Than Just
Soccer Moms:
Issues & Activism

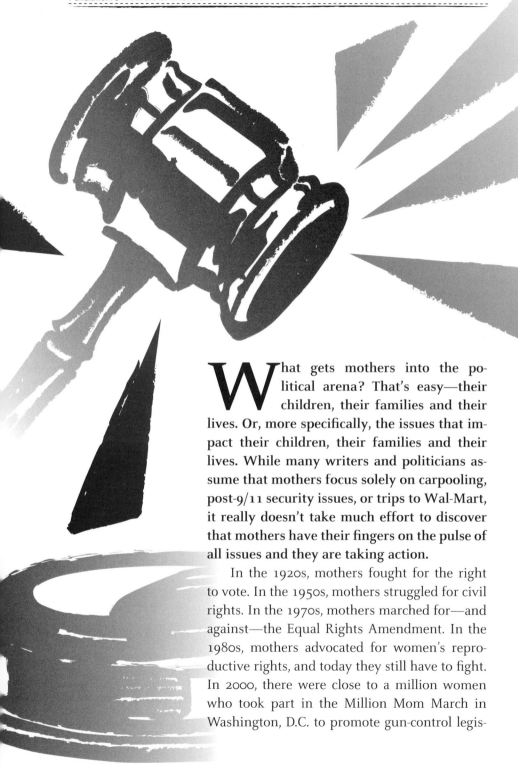

What gets mothers into the political arena? That's easy—their children, their families and their lives. Or, more specifically, the issues that impact their children, their families and their lives. While many writers and politicians assume that mothers focus solely on carpooling, post-9/11 security issues, or trips to Wal-Mart, it really doesn't take much effort to discover that mothers have their fingers on the pulse of all issues and they are taking action.

In the 1920s, mothers fought for the right to vote. In the 1950s, mothers struggled for civil rights. In the 1970s, mothers marched for—and against—the Equal Rights Amendment. In the 1980s, mothers advocated for women's reproductive rights, and today they still have to fight. In 2000, there were close to a million women who took part in the Million Mom March in Washington, D.C. to promote gun-control legislation. And in 2010, mothers like Lilly Ledbetter continued the fight for equal pay for equal work.[85] More mothers are running for elective office than ever before, and others are even starting their own political action committees.[86]

Personal issues are huge political motivators for women. With the help of new media tools, mothers' political voices are becoming more powerful on a broad range of issues that are as diverse as mothers themselves: gay rights, abortion, hunger and racism, to name a few. A war is personal if a mom is a soldier or has a child in the military. Taxes are personal when we see money being spent on programs we don't agree with. And clearly, as we have discovered since Wall Street crashed in September 2008, the economy is highly personal, especially when parents lose jobs, struggle to put food on the table, and keep a roof over their families' heads.

While women's views are never completely defined by their motherhood or any other aspect of their lives, the lens of parenting is a powerful influence that shapes our opinions and provides us with the inner fortitude to speak up about all issues that impact our families. The 2005 book *What Women Really Want*[87] debunks the long-held stereotype that politically interested mothers focus solely on "kitchen table" issues— those that impact our households directly—and reveals that mothers are equally passionate about virtually all topics politicians like to focus on, including the economy, taxes, war, and crime. But common stereotypes die hard. Even now, after mothers have led many major political efforts of the twentieth century, the media still frequently portray women with children through an antiquated June-Cleaver-meets-Mad-Men lens, with mothers as behind-the-scenes helpmates rather than independent thinkers with their own agendas for change.

Almost without exception, activist mothers I have encountered have discovered a newly sparked interest in issues and causes as a direct result of having children. Parenthood provides an instantaneous new perspective on the world, because once those children arrive, you're responsible for how the world is going to look when they're grown.[88] Research conducted after the 2008 presidential election bears that out—Barack Obama's presidential candidacy spurred mothers into the realm of political activism as never before.[89] Whether we're spearheading a community food drive or running for president of the United States, as mothers, our inspiration and motivation are frequently fueled by our families.

The concept of motherhood experiences and political activism being intertwined gained attention in 1992, when Patty Murray announced during her first bid for the United States Senate that she was "just a mom in tennis shoes." She transformed that phrase, which had once been used against her to suggest she was unqualified for public office, into a powerful connection with women voters about her concerns and sensibilities.[90] Now, almost 20 years later, politically powerful women commonly embrace motherhood as a political tool. Democratic Congresswoman Nancy Pelosi has often said that her identity as a parent was a significant motivator to become involved in politics. She embraced the imagery of that idea by surrounding herself with children, including her own grandchildren, as she took the gavel when she was sworn in as the first female Speaker of the House in 2007. In the 2010 rally-the-base movie *Fire from the Heartland: The Awakening of the Conservative Woman,* many of the conservative women activists profiled mentioned that motherhood both qualified and motivated them to get politically involved.

The phenomenon of preeminent political women showcasing their motherhood bona fides exploded after Hillary Clinton dropped out of the 2008 presidential race, which raises the question of whether subsequent candidates "went to school" on the hard lessons learned in Clinton's campaign. Clinton's closest advisors made a calculated decision to downplay her gender and parental status, and instead focus on her more "masculine" qualities of proven leadership ability and her tenure in the Senate.[91] That could have been a good call in the shoulder-pad and floppy-bow-tie era of the 1980s, but her advisors missed a cultural shift in what voters would or could respond to in 2008: being able to see a woman candidate as the sum of all the parts of her life, including children.[92] Maybe if Clinton had embraced her feminine side and brought her mother and daughter on the campaign trail early on, things would have turned out differently. It's hard to say. By the time she did, however, it was too late.

Of course, in 2010 the political mother of all political mothers was Sarah Palin, who took the iconography of political motherhood to a level never before seen in American politics. Famous for her 'I'm-a-mother-and-I-can-do-anything perspective,'[93] Palin infused her agenda with her rugged Alaskan mother status. When she saw how enthusiastically the segment of long-ignored politically conservative women responded to those references, Palin upped that motherhood ante with the creation of her conservative "mama grizzlies" meme in the 2010 midterms, [94] even highlighting her role as the queen mama grizzly in her own reality television show, *Sarah Palin's Alaska.*

Mothers don't have to mold themselves in the image of Palin or Pelosi to effect change. Using our growing influence online to craft a better future—or even a better now—for everyone's children is a concept that resonates with many mothers. We spend a lot of time wielding our maternal power to influence what our children eat, what they watch, and who they spend their time with. It's just a natural next step for us to decide we also want to find a way to have a larger impact by becoming more vocal in the world of political issues.

Leslie Sanchez, the author of *You've Come a Long Way, Maybe: Sarah, Michelle, Hillary, and the Shaping of the New American Woman,*[95] isn't surprised by the wave of activist mothers. Based on her experiences— both as a political analyst and as a girl who grew up surrounded by a community of what she describes as strong South Texas women—she knows all about what she calls "cause moms:" mothers motivated to political action by life circumstances and community events. Their involvement in the lives of their families and friends provides the focus that leads them to become political advocates.[96]

Although I find labels limiting, "cause mom" is much better than "soccer mom," "security mom," "Wal-Mart mom" or "maxed-out mom." These terms imply that mothers' interests are limited to minivan gas mileage, a desire to be protected in a post-9/11 world and trying to squeeze $1.05 out of each hard-earned dollar. I understand the need for short-hand references that encapsulate broader ideas, especially in the world of quick-hit journalism, but they are often misleading or just plain wrong.

We now know that "security moms" was more a pop-culture label than the definition of a new political constituency. There are conflicting reports about who first coined the phrase, but it was exploited by the George W. Bush 2004 presidential campaign in the hope of wooing voters.[97] While research has shown time and again that women voters are not two-dimensional creatures, the media often perpetuate terms like "soccer moms" and "security moms," rather than portray them as the multi-dimensional citizens they are.

The disparity between what women actually focus on and how their

interests are it is portrayed in the media and by candidates is supported by what journalist Melinda Henneberger found during her travels
following the 2004 presidential election. While interviewing women
for her book, *If They Only Listened to Us: What Women Voters Want
Politicians to Hear*,[98] Henneberger discovered a disconnect between what
politicians were saying America wanted and what voters—especially
women—were saying. Her curiosity led to a road trip to meet and interview women voters across the country and get their say. According to
Henneberger, all the so-called security mom voters must have gone into
hiding immediately after Bush's re-election; as she listened to women's
stories about activism and politics nationwide, she learned that most of
the women she interviewed who cast their votes based on security issues
had actually voted for John Kerry, not for George W. Bush, because of
their security concerns.[99]

While few mothers fit neatly into any of these stereotypes, it's hard
not to wonder why the media continue to create neat little boxes for the
purposes of defining us? This practice conveys an attitude that once
women become mothers, regardless of our life experience or educations,
we can be conveniently lumped together for descriptive purposes as one
big "momolith." Maybe that's because even in the run-up to the 2008
presidential election, there were still few outlets for the real opinions
and views of mothers to be expressed.

In the blogosphere, there is room for us to express ourselves and
be heard as individuals in a way we haven't before. Many women are
discovering new power by flexing their online presence to advocate for
issues, create political movements, and get all riled up in their own political ways. Women's online writing reveals that mothers are channeling their inner Howard Beale from the movie *Network*—they're mad
as hell and don't want to take it anymore. They're redefining influence
and stretching their political muscles through their increasing numbers
online and new media opportunities to speak up for issues they care
about. Traditional news outlets still give us outstanding commentary by
the likes of E.J Dionne, Bill Kristol or Maureen Dowd. But if policymakers want the real scoop, they ought to be paying attention to the activist
mothers writing about issues.

A perfect example of mothers doing just that is the story of the online community called *TheMotherhood*. In the wake of Hurricane Katrina

in 2005, Emily McKhann and Cooper Munroe, who co-authored a blog about their lives called *been there*, started a grassroots effort on their site to get needed supplies to Katrina's victims. They posted stories from the people they interviewed and listed what items people needed; they were able to coordinate an incredible effort to provide supplies that, at least initially, the federal government wasn't.[100]

Thanks to their efforts, McKhann and Munroe experienced the power of women's online activism first-hand. People were so moved by their plan to aid Katrina victims, that tens of thousands of readers rushed to their site, causing it to crash shortly after they announced their efforts. That response showed the power that storytelling could have in the online world; the next step was to figure out how to take that energy and connect in a bigger way with lawmakers to change the public discourse. So they created a new site called *TheMotherhood*, and online community that not only allowed them to continue their outreach efforts but also provided a place where lawmakers would take mothers' voices seriously and understand the need for a real conversation with them.

Similarly, another duo of dynamic mothers saw the need to create a new way to reach lawmakers on issues important to mothers. Kristin Rowe-Finkbeiner and Joan Blades co-founded the online grassroots organization *MomsRising* to promote awareness and legislative change on issues that have long seriously impacted mothers and families. Blades, the founder of the progressive political group *MoveOn.org*, partnered with Rowe-Finkbeiner, a former environmental consultant and expert on maternal discrimination,[101] to form *MomsRising*, a non-profit that now boasts over a million members.

Rowe-Finkbeiner never intended to become the leader of a large activist organization. But after she became a mother of a son born with an immune-deficiency disorder, she quickly came to understand the realities of what happens to families who don't have the social safety net she had. She was forced to leave her job to care for her son, which meant losing her family's health insurance.[102] That experience in her relatively secure household made her realize how close to the edge all families are when it comes to being able to afford health insurance. Today, Rowe-Finkbeiner travels the country, along with growing numbers of *MomsRising* advocates, to meet with high-level lawmakers like former Speaker of the House Nancy Pelosi and Senate Majority Leader Harry

Reid and keep those issues on their legislative radar. To date, Rowe-Finkbeiner says *MomsRising* members have made more than 600,000 contacts with lawmakers, both by phone and e-mail, to advocate on behalf of health-care reform legislation and other issues that impact women, children, and their families.[103]

The fact that women are finding power for change in online communities and connections is undeniable. But there is even more power if we can take our online connections into the offline world. Women are consensus builders by nature; we love our "villages," whether real or virtual. And while many of us have often been shut out of informal male networking opportunities to advance the causes women care about, I believe it's the relationships and communities we develop in the online world that will allow women to make advances in the real world. We just need to bring more women together and harness it.

To that end, women who are active online are combining those efforts with offline relationship building. In 2010, well over two 2,000 women attended the annual *BlogHer* blogging and networking conference in New York City. At *BlogHer's* 2009 event in Chicago, I attended one of the opening events with feminist pioneer and former Planned Parenthood of America president Gloria Feldt, along with hundreds of energetic women who were eating, drinking, and chatting. The decibel level in the room was overwhelming; if you wanted to have a conversation, you had to shout to be heard. ooking at all the women, Feldt turned to me and said, "There's so much power in this room."

Her comment had two meanings: first, that it was amazing so many women had come together for a conference about writing and blogging; and second, that she saw a powerful resource, one that could be developed from a social get-together to an army for change. At the same time, she also seemed a little sad—as someone who has tried to bring women together for real social change—seeing that many of those present were motivated to attend only for the free chardonnay and swag bags. They didn't realize the impact they could have if they channeled that time and energy just a bit differently.

Embracing the desire to create change usually requires something becoming intensely personal, as it did with Rowe-Finkbeiner and the women of *TheMotherhood*. Our kids need medical care. Our water isn't safe to drink. We almost lost our life because a certain medical procedure wasn't available to us. We each have to find our own way to the political world in our own time. But as more mothers write about their own personal connections and motivations, I hope it will inspire others. So that the next time we drink that chardonnay, we can also toast our inner activists.

CYNTHIA DAVIS IS RIGHT: HUNGER IS A MOTIVATOR
by Jaelithe Judy, MOMocrats blog

Missouri State Representative Cynthia Davis—a Republican from O'Fallon, a St. Louis suburb with a median income 60 percent higher than the state average—recently criticized the state of Missouri's summer free lunch program for impoverished children in her monthly newsletter, saying that "hunger can be a positive motivator" for kids. She argues that parents who have been laid off during the recession ought to be able to make do without government assistance:

> Most parents put their children first, even ahead of themselves no matter what. If parents are laid off, that doesn't mean they stop feeding their children, at least not any of the parents I know. Laid off parents could adapt by preparing more home-cooked meals rather than going out to eat.

And she maintains that if Missouri shuts down the free lunch program, children who find themselves going hungry will just be that much more motivated to feed themselves at no cost to the state by getting jobs at fast food restaurants:

> Anyone under 18 can be eligible? Can't they get a job during the summer by the time they are 16? Hunger can be a positive motivator. What is wrong with the idea of getting a job so you can get better meals?

Tip: If you work for McDonald's, they will feed you for free during your break.

No word from Ms. Davis yet on what those Missouri families who were already unable to afford regularly going out to eat *before* losing their income to recession ought to do to "adapt" to their new lack of funds to buy food. No word either on what teenagers are supposed to do if there are no jobs available at the local McDonald's because all positions there have been taken by recently laid-off adults. Or on how these kids are supposed to get to work if they cannot afford, say, a car, given that the local public transportation system recently cut bus services. No direction from Ms. Davis on what "motivated" younger children who cannot work at McDonald's are supposed to do to feed themselves.

Facing criticism by political bloggers and local and national press, Cynthia Davis continued to defend her position. I think Representative Davis is right about one thing: hunger *is* a motivator.

You never forget going hungry. *Being* hungry, well. That happens every day. As in, it's lunchtime. I'm hungry. Let's go out for a bite. I know a great little taco place down the street with fresh guacamole. That sort of feeling is commonplace. Forgettable. You don't always remember today what you ate for lunch three days ago, let alone the craving that drove you to eat in the first place.

But *going* hungry—that is a different story. That's waking up in the morning hungry. Feeling, throughout the day, hungry. Lying in bed not able to sleep just yet because you are hungry. Dreaming about feeling hungry.

And there is no trip to the taco place down the street and no trip to McDonald's instead and no a trip to the farmer's market or the grocery store, either, because there is no money for those things. There is not even the option of a trip to the backyard for some homegrown tomatoes or cucumbers or strawberries because there is no yard when you live in a run-down apartment or a shelter or a car.

There is only your hollow-eyed mother who is hungrier than you and who is dividing the last stale crackers to make them last. Assuming that you are lucky enough to have a mother. And crackers.

And the "going" part of going hungry means, of course, that you keep going this way. That despite the aching hollow in your belly and the listlessness that overtakes your brain, you do keep going— to school or to work or to the streets or at the least from one side of an empty room to another. You keep waking up in the morning and going about your day as best you can as if you were not hungry.

Because the world expects it of you, because you are ashamed to admit you are hungry, because your body holds some sort of ancient optimism that there will be food again around some corner, because, after all, what else can you do?

You don't forget going hungry, and I know that you don't forget it because I was once a hungry child and some of my earliest and most indelible memories are of going hungry. Of feeling motivated by hunger. Motivated to suck on a lone slice of pickle for hours just to keep the feeling of food in my mouth. (I can still taste that pickle when I think about it. I was four.) Motivated to think that someone else's trash smelled like food. Yes, hunger motivates people.

Hunger—especially hunger that is not just their own, but belongs to their children—motivates women to stay in abusive or unhappy relationships. Hunger motivates children to shoplift, or to drop out of school to find work that is not always safe and not always legal. Hunger, I am sure, was one of the things motivating the 16-year-old boy who once stole my purse and a bag of groceries at knifepoint in a neighborhood where I myself had once gone hungry.

Hunger motivates families to argue, and sometimes it motivates them to split up to qualify for better resources, or to split up just in order to not have to look one another in the face and see hunger. It motivates people to buy unhealthy food because it's cheaper and to binge on available food wherever they find it no matter the quality and to hoard and crave foods that are high in fat and calories, and so, ironically, hunger motivates obesity. Hunger motivates people to take drugs to forget about the threat of being hungry, or to sell drugs, in an attempt to never have to worry again about buying food.

Hunger motivates street children selling their bodies in Thailand, (does Ms. Davis consider that meaningful employment?) and hunger motivates teenage terrorists in drought-stricken Afghanistan, where decades of war have completely destroyed once-fertile farmland. Hunger motivates Mexican immigrants who risk their lives sneaking across desolate desert borders. Hunger motivates North Koreans in prison camps to sew uniforms for the army that oppresses them.

Hunger is a powerful motivator. But it is not always positive.

I would be lying if I said that my own thankfully brief experiences with childhood hunger did not motivate me to try harder in school as a potential path out of poverty. I would be lying if I said that my mother's fear of her children's hunger did not motivate her to fight her way to a better job and better wages.

But you see, it was the free school lunches I qualified for, in those early days when I was hungry, that kept enough glucose in my brain so I could pay attention in my the classroom. It was the knowledge that her children would still eat if she went back to school that allowed my high-school-dropout teenage mother to spend my early childhood finishing her college degree instead of working at McDonald's. State-sponsored food, given to me at a crucial time by the fine state of Missouri, helped lift my family out of poverty.

Being saved from hunger can be a positive motivator for children. As soon as I was old enough to realize what a debt of gratitude I owed my neighbors, I felt motivated to pay it back in part by working to prevent *their* children from having to go hungry. By donating to food pantries. By promoting hunger awareness programs. By growing, once I had a yard to grow food in, more tomatoes and beans than my own family could possibly eat and walking up and down my mostly working-class street handing fresh produce out to my neighbors for the past three summers. By figuring out without asking which of my neighbors have been visiting the food pantry since the recession hit and having healthy snacks on hand every time the children from those houses visit my house.

By voting in favor of funding to improve schools and school lunch programs. By voting to raise my own taxes (and yes, contrary to popular conservative belief about bleeding heart liberals, I do work, and I do pay taxes) to secure the welfare of my home state's children. By campaigning for candidates who share my view that no child in the United States of America should have to go hungry while we as a nation have an overabundance of food.

By campaigning *against* politicians like Cynthia Davis.

Hunger motivates people to do many things. But I think the most positive thing hunger has ever motivated me to do is to try to prevent other people from having to experience hunger.

Hunger is motivating me right now to write these words and

that is why it is not the college-educated, professional, home-owning middle-class woman with a stable family and a full pantry who considers you now, Cynthia Davis, but the four-year-old girl whose memory lives inside me, for whom none of that blissfully food-secure future has yet been decided.

She thinks that you're being mean and scary and that you should not be allowed to make important decisions about the lives of a state full of children.

She also hopes your own children never have to know what it feels like to go hungry.

WHY I'M PRO-LIFE
by Shannon Lowe, Rocks in My Dryer blog

I wasn't always pro-life.

In the early '90s, I was a card-carrying, sign-waving, Bill Clinton-campaigning pro-choicer. I held to the notion that a fetus couldn't fully be life, since it was dependent entirely on another for its existence. And I believed the notion that abortion is unfortunate, but it wasn't any of the government's business.

I wish I could point you to a specific point on my journey where my views shifted entirely. There was no dramatic morning where I woke up suddenly pro-life. My thoughts on the subject have meandered down many roads before winding up where they are today. I've been asked to tell you why I believe the way I do.

I will, and I invite you to come to this conversation with respect and courtesy. There's too much yelling over this issue, on both sides, making it impossible to hear each other. I understand (because I've been there) that pro-choicers stand by their position firmly because they believe they're defending the fundamental value of *choice*.

And I understand (because I'm there *now*) that pro-lifers stand by their position firmly because they believe they're defending the fundamental value of *life*.

Volumes and volumes have been written on the subject, and smarter people than I have debated it for years. Time and space will not allow for me to address every imaginable facet of this debate.

But I will address the two issues that ultimately were responsible for changing my heart on the subject of abortion: that of an embryo/fetus as life, and the issue of choice.

The embryo and fetus as life

I'm no scientist, but I pay enough attention to know that defining life is no black-and-white matter. For many years, I made myself comfortable with the definition of life as that which could be sustained independently from another human.

It was a tidy argument, I thought, until I began to expand it outward. If only independently sustainable life really "counted" then what would we do with the Alzheimer's patient who would wander off into danger without constant supervision? Or the mentally disabled child who could not eat without being fed by someone else? Or the young mother dependent on dialysis for survival?

By my old definition, I was discrediting the "alive-ness" of people who needed help to exist. The slope was so terribly slippery that I found myself flailing as I slipped down it. If I could no longer consider dependence on another a pre-requisite for being human, then where would I draw the line? Science seemed to be making things more ambiguous, but my heart craved a more concrete answer. After reading and looking, investigating and comparing, I realized I had to admit to myself there was only one unambiguous start of life that satisfied me:

Conception.

But there was that slippery slope again. Where did this put that important issue of a woman's right to choose?

The issue of choice

Choice is a beautiful thing. It is a fundamental part of what makes us humans. I passionately defend a woman's right to choose a career or schooling or housing or any number of life avenues. I defend her choice to decide whether to have sex, and with whom, and how often, and whether or not to use birth control.

But absolute, unhindered choice is not a guaranteed human right. Think about it: civil society already tells us that we cannot "choose" to abuse a child or "choose" to steal a car. There are legal consequences to those actions, because "choosing" to burglarize a home infringes on the basic liberties of the person who lives there.

The precedent is set. *When our right to choose bumps up against the right of another to exist peacefully, our choice is blocked by civilized law.*

And it is with this in mind that I realized, as I came to terms with the validity of the human-ness of an embryo and fetus, that I had to accept there was a moral point at which a "woman's right to choose" ended. Her right to decide what to do with her body bumps up against the right of that baby's right to exist.

The only place I could arrive after looking at the medical, legal, social, civil, and constitutional issues was that *something had to give.* A woman's right to choose an abortion cannot logically co-exist with an embryo's or a fetus' right to be born.

Simply put, *life* trumps *choice.*

And no, to answer the question that inevitably arises when this issue is brought up, I don't think the pro-life movement is perfect (then again, is *any* movement?). I cannot be responsible for every-thing every pro-lifer does, but I can be responsible for what goes on in my own heart and head. I recognize that crisis pregnancies are very real and very serious, and pro-lifers who dismiss the anguish of such situations are unkind and naive. We, as pro-lifers, should be at the forefront of helping women, in very practical ways, navigate unplanned and crisis pregnancies. Many pro-lifers, to their credit, already do this. More should.

Perhaps, if both sides of this debate stopped shouting, we could better focus on the people at the heart of the issues: babies and pregnant women. Both deserve our respect and our best ef-forts to help them live with dignity.

SPEAKING TO THE CANDIDATES ABOUT CHOICE
by Cecily Kellogg, Uppercase Woman blog

Apparently, some folks who read my blog know some folks who know some folks who swear they can get this blog entry read by

Barack Obama. But I figured, why limit myself to just writing to one presidential candidate? I'm speaking to everyone including Hillary Clinton and John McCain (okay, maybe not Ralph Nader).

Why have I been appointed as someone to discuss the issue of choice? Because I'm the Internet Poster Girl for Partial Birth Abortion, that's why. It's not a title I'm proud of, but it's one I was saddled with a few years ago.

I'm not going to get into the whole story, but I'll give you the short version. In April 2004, I was lucky enough to get pregnant with twin boys after undergoing in vitro treatment for male-factor infertility (thanks to drugs my husband's mother took—DES, we suspect—while she was pregnant with him). We were on top of the world, although the pregnancy was difficult.

But a routine ultrasound—meant to be a time of great joy—revealed terrible news: one of the twins had died, probably about a week before. We went from the ultrasound appointment to my obstetrician's office and were met with even more grim news. My weight had spiked up about 18 pounds, my blood pressure was soaring, and I had protein in my urine.

It turned out that I was in full-blown preeclampsia. I was admitted to the hospital immediately.

After that, everything happened very quickly. I was put on medication (magnesium sulfate) in an attempt to treat the preeclampsia and save the remaining twin until he reached outside-the-womb viability—a mere two weeks away (I was just over 22 weeks pregnant). But I got much worse overnight; my blood pressure couldn't be controlled, I had a massive headache and was vomiting uncontrollably. My kidneys shut down. I was moments away from seizures, coma, and death when the doctors came and told us the bad news: my remaining twin could not be saved. My pregnancy had to be terminated, or both the baby and I would die.

You might, Mr. Obama and Mr. McCain, be able to imagine what it felt like to be my husband—to imagine being terrified of losing your children and your wife in one fell swoop. Ms. Clinton, you might be able to imagine lying in the hospital, so sick you barely feel any of what is happening, only knowing that the long-fought-for children you so desperately wanted are now both going to be dead.

Here's the part of the story where choice comes in. I could, of course, have gone through induced labor and delivered my tiny twins. But my blood pressure was hovering around 165/120 (often going higher), even with treatment. Can you imagine what labor would have done to my body with blood pressure that high? My doctor recommended, and I agreed, that I undergo the much less stressful intact dilation and extraction procedure—what the "pro-life" forces often like to call a "partial birth abortion." Of course, you being the smart and well-educated politicians that you are know that there is NO medical procedure that is *actually* called a "partial birth abortion," so you know that there are several medical procedures that the "pro-life" movement put in that category, including the one that I had. Wait, I take that back—Mr. McCain, as you have been a staunch supporter of the Partial Birth Abortion ban, you clearly were asleep in class when they discussed the actual procedures.

But I digress. My doctor refers to my procedure as the worst moment in his professional career. As I lay on the gurney, waiting for my procedure to start, I felt a gulf of grief and emptiness the likes of which I have never known. I felt abandoned by God. I lay there, crying, alone, surrounded by doctors and nurses. You can't imagine the sadness.

Trust me when I tell you that it was the very worst day of my life.

But I was lucky. Are you surprised that I would say that? I was lucky because the partial-birth abortion ban was not yet in effect in October 2004. If it had been, I would have been forced to undergo labor and delivery, no matter the risks to my health, and I might right now be either dead or so brain damaged I would be unable to type this. I was additionally lucky because even though I live in Philadelphia, one of the largest cities in the country, my doctor happened to be only *one of two doctors in this entire city* that was willing and able to perform this life-saving medical procedure (although he can't now, of course, thanks to the ban being enacted).

So that's my story. For a year after that, I licked my wounds and missed my sons, Nicholas and Zachary. Eventually, I underwent a frozen embryo transfer and gave birth to my daughter Victoria, whose grinning face you can see at my blog. I had problems with her delivery as well, so I will not be having other children, sadly.

I'm sure that you will find my story compelling. Even the most hard-hearted and most staunch pro-lifers have. Many who came to my blog to question my decision have stayed and become friends. You know why? Because mine was an "acceptable" abortion. I'm not a 26-year-old professional woman who doesn't want to derail her career by having a child and chooses to terminate a pregnancy. Or a teenage girl who got drunk and forgot to make the boy wear a condom. Or a harried mother of three who just can't imagine having a fourth child.

So it's easy to read my story and say, 'Oh, yes, in cases *like yours*, abortion should be legal.' But when laws are passed that make it difficult for that teenage girl to exercise the right to control her own body—hey, I'm looking at you, Ms. Clinton, for not standing up harder against the parental notification laws—or for the professional woman or the harried mother to be able to fill a prescription, quietly, for RU486 at her local pharmacy so she can make her choice as well—when those laws are passed, it's women like me that die. When you cut corners, you don't save babies' lives. You kill women like me.

Let me say that again. When you compromise on abortion—when you sacrifice even the smallest corner of choice—you kill women like me. You create a culture of fear among doctors that puts lives like mine at risk.

By banning these medical procedures, they are taking a medical decision out of the hands of the people involved—the patient and the doctor—and putting it in the hands of legislators, most of whom have no medical training. Some hospitals now require panels of doctors and lawyers to be convened to review cases where a late-term termination is recommended. If that had been required in my case well, I would have likely suffered far greater damage to my health and quality of life, possibly permanent, while they wrangled over the legal implications of saving me.

So knock it off, will you? Fight to protect a woman's right to choose. I know, Ms. Clinton, that you believe in it enough to put it on the front page of your website, but your record isn't perfect.

Mr. Obama, you do not discuss choice on your campaign page (although it's hosted on the Women for Obama page). Why not? Mr. McCain, for shame. Shame on you for promoting a law that is basically a warrant for my death. Come on.

I'm tired of writing about this. I am tired of being the Internet Poster Girl for Partial Birth Abortion, I assure you. It's not comfortable. By writing this, I will get a new batch of pro-life people that will start telling me how I murdered my sons, how they could have lived (they never, ever, remember that one had already passed away), and some will threaten me. It happens every time I talk about this. Sometimes I just want to lie down and let someone else do this. But I won't. I don't know what it will take, perhaps a constitutional amendment protecting women's bodies?

Yeah. That might do it. Sigh. Like that will ever happen.

WALL STREET ISN'T AFRAID OF THE SEC
by Joanne Bamberger, PunditMom blog

You might say I have a little inside information about the Securities and Exchange Commission.

I spent several years there before I was a "recovering attorney"—first as lawyer in the Enforcement Division investigating a variety of securities fraud cases and then as Deputy Director of Public Affairs, where I dealt with reporters all day long about cases being brought and how the agency worked. Granted, it's been a few years since I walked around the halls of the agency known as the Investor's Advocate, but my guess is that for the most part things aren't so different. Except that this relatively small government agency has become everyone's favorite whipping boy since the economy went into a tailspin.

But as cable news shows and newspaper headlines focus on Wall Street reform, Goldman Sachs, the mortgage crisis and the economy (that still isn't so fine, thank you very much), I just wanted to weigh in on why the mess we're in is less the fault of the SEC than of the lawmakers who are all pounding their fists, wanting you to believe that either they're trying to change the status quo or that changing that status quo will only make things worse. The real problem is this:

Wall Street isn't afraid of the SEC.

They never have been and never will be as long as the agency is structured as one that brings only civil, not criminal, cases. The handful of men who run our nation's investment banking institutions aren't afraid of consequences that they consider to be mere slaps on the hand from an inconsequential agency. The SEC can only take money from these Masters of the Universe. These guys make gobs of it all day, every day and know that they'll make more tomorrow. Can you say credit default swaps? Losing a little money is just a cost of doing business to them, so you can't even get their attention unless you can take away their ability to make more. Like when you say the word 'prison.' And the only ones who can bring criminal charges against them are the Justice Department and state Attorneys General.

The SEC might find a case and investigate it. The SEC might be the agency that does all the grunt work when it comes to digging for the dirt. But it can only stand by at the photo op when the criminal authorities start talking about the big house.

Think about it in this smaller, non-investment banking securities case—do you really think Martha Stewart batted an eyelash over her $30,000 fine after alleged insider trading? Or do you think she was more concerned about what five months in the slammer would do to her reputation, her business, and the stock price of Martha Stewart Living Omnimedia?

So when it comes to the fraud currently alleged against Goldman Sachs—and cases that the SEC investigates every day—is it any wonder that the Richard Fulds or the Lloyd Blankfeins of the investment world treat SEC investigations with about the same amount of disdain as they would a pesky mosquito?

The Securities and Exchange Commission has the authority to subpoena documents and testimony, but corporations can and do drag their feet for years to delay any actions. This tactic is a good one for those being investigated, because Wall Street also knows that: (1) it takes forever to enforce those subpoenas, and (2) that there's a lot of staff turnover at the SEC. Corporations and Wall

Street big wigs know that a staff attorney there is like the weather—if you don't like it, you don't have to wait too long for it to change. And when underpaid staff attorneys leave to seek their fortune at a big law firm or one of those Wall Street banks—a new attorney inherits an old case they usually couldn't care less about.

Unless and until the SEC can find a way to instill some fear when it comes to enforcing the nation's securities laws, few will believe there's much to lose by failing to cooperate when civil cases are filed. It's a Wall Street mindset that's existed as we've moved from *Den of Thieves* to *Liar's Poker* to the Internet trading bubble to today's mortgage investment crisis described in *The Big Short*. Not to mention that when major investment banks are big contributors to lawmakers' campaigns and former Goldman executives get plum jobs in the government, it doesn't seem likely that there will be any fear on Wall Street in the near future.

That's probably good news for Gordon Gekko and his real life counterparts.

WHAT I TOLD MY STATE SENATE ABOUT BPA
by Lisa Frack, MomsRising blog

I never thought I'd say, "I had fun testifying in Salem," but I did. Especially after hearing industry lobbyist after industry lobbyist spin the story about Bisphenol A or BPA. Yesterday I made the trip to Salem to speak in favor of a proposed ban on BPA in children's food and drink containers.

I was one of many who testified to support this bill, among them the Oregon Environmental Council, Oregon Nurses Association, and Children First for Oregon. Here's what I said:

> Chair Dingfelder, Members of the Committee, thank you for the opportunity to testify today to show my strong support for Senate Bill 1032. I'm thrilled that my state is among those stepping up to protect its children from this toxic chemical. My name is Lisa Frack. I am an Oregonian and a parent of two children under seven, both native Oregonians. Coleman

(who is seven) and Georgia (she's three) were almost certainly born with BPA in their bodies and were further contaminated in their earliest years by drinking from tainted polycarbonate baby bottles and sippy cups, and eating canned foods. That I fed them.

Our toxics laws have failed them, and failed me as a parent whose highest purpose is the health and safety of my children. Which is why I am here today.

As you've no doubt heard, the science around BPA is more solid every day. We all know it's in us, there's no question about that anymore. And while some (amazingly) continue to question its health effects, they must not be looking at the mounting scientific evidence. I'm hardly alone in feeling frustrated that my kids continue to be guinea pigs while the government and industry duke it out and do more studies. We don't need more studies, we need common sense health protective policies that put children first.

In the meantime, we parents are left holding the bag. In January, the U.S. FDA concluded that it had "some concern" about BPA and actually advised parents to take steps to minimize exposures. As you might imagine, identifying what does and doesn't contain BPA is no easy feat—especially in the grocery store aisle with two little kids in the cart. I want to buy food and drinks for my kids without wondering if the container is toxic. Is that too much to ask? I bet retailers would be thrilled if we parents would stop asking a million questions and start buying what's on their shelves again. Especially in this economic climate, they need our trust, because they need our business.

And I don't know about you, but the fact that the FDA assigned the very same level of concern to fetal exposure to amphetamines as they did to BPA alarms me as a parent, and makes it clear how badly SB 1032 is needed, because right here in Salem is where my children are going to be protected. Isn't it?

In closing, I want to leave you with another parent's perspective. Last night I mentioned to her that I'd be here today, and here's what she said, "I knew BPA was bad a long time ago, but my husband kept saying if it were, the government would protect us." Well it is bad, and the government hasn't protected us. Yet. I'm here to ask you to change that by passing this bill. Thank you.

GAYS ARE A BIGGER THREAT THAN TERRORISTS
by Amy Oztan, Selfish Mom blog

Gays are a bigger threat than terrorists. Yup, that's what Oklahoma State House Representative Sally Kern said to fellow Republicans in a speech that showed up on YouTube.

Thank God for YouTube. I mean, really, as recently as five or 10 years ago, a politician could go around saying outrageous, bigoted, crazy, hateful things to small groups of people, and not much would happen. But now, all it takes is someone with a cell phone and suddenly the whole world starts to understand just what's going on out there in city councils and state governments. It becomes a little clearer why tens of millions of people would rather vote for a moron for president—twice—than risk electing someone who just might show compassion for people who, gasp, don't live the same kind of lifestyle that they do.

"What is wrong with me, as an American, exercising my free speech rights?" said Kern in a local news interview. "I have never spoken in hate against them—never would, never will. Nor will I ever apologize for anything I said."

I'm all for differing opinions, and debate, if at the end of the day you get to live your life and I get to live mine. But once laws and politicians enter the picture, then it's not just opinion, it's not just live-and-let-live, and you don't get to be a gay-bashing bigot and hide behind free speech.

She claims that she doesn't hate them, but she thinks that the "gay agenda" will be the downfall of our entire nation. Doesn't exactly sound like a love fest to me, but OK, let's take her at her word that she doesn't hate homosexuals. What is undeniable, however, is that her words, and more importantly the laws that she has the ability to pass, have great consequences, and that is what is wrong with her exercising her free speech rights. If she doesn't hate homosexuals, she sure as hell has the opportunity to inspire people who do, people who look to their leaders for guidance.

Perhaps the scariest thing she said in the entire speech was that she had been a school teacher for more than 20 years! She helped to shape young, impressionable minds! And as a legislator, she tried (unsuccessfully) to get a bill passed that would ban libraries from carrying books in their children's sections that had gay themes.

Sally Kern is standing behind her comments. She says that those comments were made by her on at least four occasions publicly, so she isn't even sure when the Gay and Lesbian Victory Fund recorded her.

"The homosexual agenda is destroying this nation, OK, it's just a fact. Studies show no society that has totally embraced homosexuality has lasted, you know, more than a few decades. So it's the death knell in this country...I honestly think it's the biggest threat that our nation has, even more so than terrorism or Islam, which I think is a big threat," Kern said.

Kern claims that in her speech, she was not talking about individual gay people, but rather the "homosexual agenda." She seriously believes that groups' efforts to get openly gay people elected to public office will be the end of the United States of America. But besides being asinine, her words hurt. They especially hurt a young man named Tucker, who lost his mother in the Oklahoma City bombing. But out of his hurt came a response more eloquent than anything that I will ever write.

I have no idea if Tucker exists. I haven't found any evidence that his letter is a fake. But real or not, it makes its point. The end of the letter that had me in tears:

"I wish you could've met my mom. Maybe she could've guided you in how a real Christian should be acting and speaking.

"I have not had a mother for nearly 13 years now and wonder if there were fewer people like you around, people with more love and tolerance in their hearts instead of strife, if my mom would be here to watch me graduate from high school this spring. Now she won't be there. So I'll be packing my things and leaving Oklahoma to go to college elsewhere and one day be a writer, and I have no intentions to ever return here. I have no doubt that people like you will incite crazy people to build more bombs and kill more people again. I don't want to be here for that. I just can't go through that again.

"You may just see me as a kid, but let me try to teach you something. The old saying is sticks and stones will break your bones, but words will never hurt you. Well, your words hurt me. Your words disrespected the memory of my mom. Your words can cause others to pick up sticks and stones and hurt others."

My kids both have friends who have two mommies. My sister is gay. My husband's good friend, whom the kids refer to as their uncle, is gay. I'm glad that my kids will grow up thinking that this is a normal occurrence rather than an aberration. I'm glad that they've gotten to know these people first as people, without any labels. Because when they're older and they start asking questions, then maybe their automatic, knee-jerk, gut reaction to people like Sally Kern will be "WTF?"

ABOUT AFGHANISTAN...
by Karoli Kuns, odd time signatures blog

I've been reading and brain-picking for months on this topic, trying to understand it and trying to come up with how I feel about the possibility of making a longer-term commitment to a country that is known to consume empires. It's more than theoretical to me—a close relative spent a good chunk of his Foreign Service career in Kabul at some key historical touch points over the past 30 years.

I've read and I've read and I've read. I've read personal accounts of people who were not military, like Rory Stewart's tale of walking across Afghanistan, encountering the hostile, the brave and the canine. I've read intelligence reports from the past and the recent present, think-tank studies and book excerpts. And of course, I've asked people like my relative what they think. After all of that, here's what I know:

- The Bush administration did an extraordinary job of committing human and monetary resources to Afghanistan without a plan and without a real commitment to the little they did promise in 2001. Because Afghanistan became Iraq's red-headed stepchild, opportunities to keep our promises to our coalition partners and the Afghan people were lost, perhaps forever.
- Afghanistan is not Vietnam. Iraq is more analogous to Vietnam than Afghanistan is.
- Afghanistan's opium trade exceeds all other national gross domestic products and is rising at an exponential rate.
- The Pakistani Taliban pose a greater threat to Afghanistan's (and the world's for that matter) security than the Afghan Taliban. While they remain Pakistan's problem, a weak Afghanistan guarantees a more difficult road for the Pakistani government to maintain peace and order in their own country. Since Pakistan is a nuclear state, the Pakistani Taliban pose a threat to world security and the nuclear balance of power.
- The Afghan people continue to suffer from the ravages of war. Women are oppressed, poverty abounds, and the opium economy benefits criminals inside and outside the country with very little reward for the people.

I have been staunchly anti-war all of my life. I protested when we went to Afghanistan because I knew it would be a long-term commitment. I didn't expect that it would become the ignored side stage to the larger circus in Iraq, though. Now that it is slowly easing its way back to center stage, I can't simply state flatly that we should get our troops the heck out of there.

The only thing I've been able to conclude with any degree of certainty is that I'm grateful I'm not President Obama. I would not want to have to face a decision that has no immediate good news for anyone.

Here is my dilemma:

Leaving Afghanistan means leaving a country with a weak government, which will likely topple just as it has in the past. Only this time, a government overthrow could easily place the Taliban back in power like bacteria that has mutated from abortive antibiotic treatment. It comes back stronger and harder to eradicate the second time around, with the possibility of a more lethal result.

Leaving Afghanistan means sanctioning a thriving illegal opium market as the primary economic driver in their country.

Leaving Afghanistan means leaving men, women, and children in extreme poverty with no real defense against those who exploit them.

Leaving Afghanistan means abandoning all hope of the possibility of helping to build a nation that can actually survive the regional and internal conflicts that have torn it apart in the past.

Leaving Afghanistan means breaking promises we made when we sent our troops there.

I'm sure my fellow progressives and Democrats will demand my card at the door for the conflict I'm feeling over this. From everything I read, their answer is to get out and stay out, that it's a losing proposition and we're better off cutting our losses and moving on.

The problem I have? Accepting the idea that while it's fine to pay verbal service to the poverty and genocide in the world, we're unwilling to make a sacrifice to actually help end it. Our fight in Afghanistan doesn't seem to be a fight for domination of their country, but for stabilization and a pathway to a self-sufficient, self-governing Afghan state.

Mostly, though, I just have questions and more questions, with very little in the way of an absolute sense of what the best way to proceed really is.

Talk me down. Leave a comment. Tell me why I'm wrong, or right, or full of it, or just another bleeding heart liberal with no sense of practical action. I have no answers, so you'll either answer my questions or you'll raise more.

BARACK OBAMA WINS MISSISSIPPI: RACE PLAYS MAJOR ROLE IN VOTING
by Kristen Chase, MOMocrats blog

If we were wondering if race was going to play a role in the Democratic presidential primaries in 2008, then we should thank the Mississippi primary for firming it up in our minds. Am I saying that Barack Obama's policies or, heck, his inspirational speeches, were not the deciding factor for the state's fine residents, but rather that voting could have actually come down to skin color alone?

Yes. I am.

Sadly, it's not surprising. As a five-year resident of Mississippi, and a former professor at the Mississippi university Obama spoke at during the campaign, there's no doubt in my mind that Obama won based on race. Fortunately, he was a viable candidate with much to offer this country *(this coming from a Hillary supporter)*.

We're all racists at one level or another, so really, it should not surprise us. We want to believe that race doesn't drive us. And for many of us, it does not. Well, most of the time.

But for the residents of Mississippi, I truly believe it does. Working and living in the poorest state of the Union, I experienced firsthand the racial issues that we all thought (or at least hoped) were dead. White students openly expressing their fear of black students. Black students congregating together in the back of my classrooms with no one but me pointing it out. And both groups of students accepting the local high school's separate black and white homecoming court and offering their disdain for "mixed" couples.

Shocking to us? *Yes.* Everyday life in Mississippi? *Absolutely.*

Throughout the campaign I wondered how voting in the South would go, not only due to the vibrant racial tensions still alive and well, but due to the perpetuation of misogyny, as well.

I've sat in rooms with parents of my students in which the fathers would not talk to me. I had three of my ten incoming freshmen (17-year-olds!) leave my class to get married and become housewives. And I had way too many come talk to me asking what constitutes "abuse" from their significant others.

I agree that we shouldn't play "which is worse" when it comes to gender or race. But while I disagree with the intention and aim of Geraldine Ferraro's comment that Obama wouldn't have been in the presidential running if he had been a white man or a woman of any color with the same resume, I do believe she has a valid point when she said "It's okay to be sexist in some people's minds. It's not okay to be racist."

We can chalk the reasoning up to "the white man's" guilt from years of oppression, or that racial issues (for the most part) have been brought to the forefront due to various newsworthy situations (some promising, some gruesome). But race, for the most part, is cut and dry; jokes about anything related to race—language, appearance, and stereotypical behaviors—are totally off limits. Deplorable. Unacceptable.

But gender is a whole other story, and from what I've seen, it holds way too many loopholes and nuances that people have taken advantage of in this particular race.

However, when it came down to Mississippi, racism won. Although, we'll never really know since there were only two choices on the ballot.

THE BODY OF THE DOCTOR
by Deborah Quinn, MaNNaHaTTaMaMMa blog

There is a vigil happening right now in Union Square for Dr. George Tiller, the doctor who was shot *in a church* in Kansas. One of the few doctors who still performed late-term abortions for women who needed them. I can't go to the vigil because I'm home, making dinner for my very desired, very *wanted* children, who I can afford to feed and clothe, as well as supply (sometimes)with Legos, Bakugan, Hot Wheels, and swimming lessons.

A (very long) while back, I was having dinner with four of my closest friends from college and we realized that in our college years (and the few years immediately after college), among the five of us, we had had four abortions, two incidents of date rape, and a wide array of unsavory and unsatisfying boyfriends. Through nothing but sheer dumb luck, I was not one of the women who had an abortion.

Instead, I drove friends to the clinic, waited with them, and drove them home. But those roles could have easily been reversed; I could have been the passenger, not the driver.

Now all of us are mothers—of babies we had inside the shelter created bystable relationships, jobs, health insurance, and family support.

But if we'd been forced to carry those college-created babies to term, who knows what would have happened to those unwanted children, the products of broken condoms, drunken fumblings, "true love" that didn't last. And who knows what would have happened to us, women not ready to be mothers?

What I do know is that more than twenty years ago, we had access to a safe, clean, *close* clinic that helped us through those dark hours. It never occurred to us, way back when, that twenty years later those pro-life protesters would still be shaking their horrific posters at women caught in the most difficult decision of their lives. How does a "pro-life" agenda square with shooting a man in cold blood, in a church? The idea of violence in a church violates the very foundations of social order, even if, for me, "faith" isn't a daily part of life.

A few years ago, Bill McKibben wrote an article in *Harper's*, called "The Christian Paradox: How A Faithful Nation Gets Jesus Wrong," in which he pointed out that the most basic precept of Christianity is the truly radical notion of "love thy neighbor as thyself." And it is radical. I mean, think about it—if you love your neighbor as yourself, can you imagine telling that person who (not) to marry? Or how to educate her children? Or what to do with her own body?

Somewhere in the fringes of the "pro-life" movement (and one must use quotation here, because let's be frank—there seems to be a real confusion about whose lives are and are not valued), there are people who are applauding what happened in Kansas. How they rationalize this act of violence with their putative faith, I don't know.

I do know that there are many people of faith, including many Catholics, who are outraged by what happened, and who knows, maybe—*finally*—Dr. Tiller's death will be the catalyst that moves us closer to that radical and foundational Christian notion of loving our neighbors. But I have to say that I'm not optimistic.

The vigil in Union Square is over now; I can see from my window that people are filing home, and I suppose that some of the women in the crowd are themselves wrestling with the dilemma my friends wrestled with, decades ago.

How can it be that all these years later, we are having the same battle over women's bodies? And how can it be that women have even *fewer* resources than we did then? And how can it be that the body of a doctor—a healer—has so little value?

A doctor killed in a church. How do we put that statement next to the phrase "a civilized society?"

MICHELE BACHMANN'S TEA PARTY CAUCUS – I JUST SAY NO
by Kim Jossfolk, Just a Conservative Girl blog

In 2010, former Speaker of the House Nancy Pelosi gave her seal of approval for the creation of the Tea Party Caucus in the House of Representatives. That is wonderful, right? I think not. I don't in any way think that Congresswoman Michele Bachmann, who is the chairwoman of that caucus, is not committed to conservative principles; I truly believe that she is. That is not the issue. The issue is does the Tea Party want to become just another lobbying group?

The beauty of the Tea Party, as I see it, is the grassroots movement of it all. I am not naïve enough to believe that there are not corporate sponsors and some people pulling strings behind the scenes. But for the most part, the movement is about people who are worried about the type of country we are leaving for our children and grandchildren. People who put up their own money to travel to different events, buy books on the Constitution and the founding of our country, and have informed themselves on legislation and how Congress works.

Being located in the Washington, D.C. area, I have had the pleasure of attending virtually all the Tea Party events about the healthcare reform law. I personally met Michele Bachmann on two occasions. I believe that she is very committed to ridding our government of big spending policies that fall outside the purview of the constitutional powers of the federal government, and would like to see more power returned to the states where they rightly belong.

One of the things that attracted me to the Tea Party movement is the fact that people are standing up and saying "no" to an out-of-control federal government. So many of us have been screaming at our televisions for years now, but didn't do much else. We have actually gotten up off our couches and have started doing things about it.

But the Tea Party movement needs to stay away from too closely aligning itself to any one politician or to one party. I realize that Democrats are not, for the most part, willing to align themselves with the Tea Party movement, nor do they really care about the same issues that we do, but that isn't a good enough reason to align ourselves to politicians who have not proven to stand by these principles once they have the majority.

One of the main reasons we have this far left trifecta is because of the irresponsible behavior of the Republicans when President Bush was spending money like a drunken sailor. So why should we trust the Republicans now? I am still not so sure that they have learned the lessons, and the entire country is suffering due to their own overspending. I don't think we should so easily allow the Republican Party to hijack this movement. They have yet to earn it.

AND I THOUGHT I WAS DONE
by Elizabeth Aquino, a moon, worn as if it had been a shell blog

I thought I was done. I really did. I wanted to be done. I was going to go back to posting about my crazy life with the disabled daughter, the absurdity of living with someone you love and not being able to really help her, fix her, make her stop having seizures. I was going to go back to posting poetry, idle musings about mindfulness, the beauty of the everyday, and yoga. I even started a food blog!

And then I talked, briefly, *TO MY MOTHER*. I love my mother, I really do. She is a wonderful mother, full of love and enthusiasm. As a child, I always felt safe and I always felt loved. But my mother is an ardent conservative and has grown increasingly so as she's gotten older. In fact, *ardent* might be an understatement.She listens to Rush Limbaugh and is, frankly, immovable(I guess the apple doesn't fall far from the tree?). She is ideological to the core and such is the nature of our political discourse (think fiery, think pyrotechnics like you've never seen, think Civil War and brother fighting brother) that we're better off not talking about much of anything of substance at all. My father is a tad more moderate than she and a lot more reasoned, but I'd actually rather not engage him in political discourse, either, other than the sharing of articles that we read, because, well– I'll boil it down to this: ***NEVER THE TWAIN SHALL MEET.***

When my sister recently shared with me that our parents were going to be traveling to Washington, D.C. to pay her a visit and also to go to an anti-Obamacare rally with a few other couples (and who knows how many other people), I brushed it off. I didn't want to think about it. In fact, I really blocked it from my mind and forgot about it. But tonight, when my mother called and started to tell me what she was doing this weekend, I had to hang up the phone. Even typing this makes me feel shaky and almost sick to my stomach, eight hours later. I know she detected something in my voice, because she's good at that. But I said my civil good-bye and hung up.

It's difficult to parse out these feelings and make sense of them. I believe in honoring one's mother and father. And I'm bound to them, inextricably, the ties made of not just duty, but love and respect for who they are and what they've made of their lives. So much is at stake, I guess. This isn't just the usual disagreement about Republicans and Democrats, liberal versus conservative, etc., etc. For me, this issue is intensely personal and, while I don't expect the rest of the country to feel the same way that I do about what's happening with health-care reform, I wish that my parents would, at the very least, be sensitive to what this means for us. For Sophie. Because the facts, for us, are not about Obamacare and the "slippery slope to socialism." The facts are that we have a daughter whose chronic health-care needs have caused not only grief and anxiety and panic and devastation and depression and near-bankruptcy, but that the health care industry, as it exists now, has contributed greatly and, in some cases, caused this.

I am being intensely personal now, knowing full well that there are tens of thousands, if not millions of people like us, of children like Sophie. And more than half the reason I fight for health-care reform and for health-care quality for all is for those other children. But when I read that I might have to buy into a special insurance pool, run by private enterprise, to get health insurance for my daughter (one of the concessions made, under pressure by politicians under the stranglehold of private enterprise, namely insurance), I feel profoundly depressed and anxious. I think, *What is going to happen to us?* And *us,* in this particular instance, means *us,* The Husband, Sophie, my two boys and myself.

I had felt a glimmer of hope when this whole health-care reform initiative started, and let me tell you, it's the hope that can sustain you if you have a child with a disability and have fought some insurance battles before, if a bed for said child is taken away at a prestigious hospital because there aren't enough and the nurse who tells you this news answers your question, *If Madonna needed a bed for her seizing daughter, would she get one?* and the answer is *YES.* You feel hope that there's going to be a change from the times you've had to fax prescriptions to Canada and London to get your hands on a drug that is too expensive for the FDA to look into approving but still costs you over $300 a month. You feel hope about a CHANGE when you hear that drug companies make grotesque profits marketing their wares on television, interfering with the sanctity of doctor/patient relationships, creating dependencies and, in some cases, illness itself. I felt hope.

When I hear and know that my parents are going to support this kind of thing, the fighting of this CHANGE well, I feel defeated. And broken-hearted. And that, too, is an understatement. And that's why I can't speak to my mother, at least about her weekend rally. It's not about her right to protest something. It's much bigger because this protest is against people like me. Like my husband and our sons. Like Sophie.

I now understand, a bit, the intensity of feelings that caused cousin to fight cousin and perhaps brother to fight brother during this country's terrible Civil War. It's a strange empathy and distinctly uncomfortable. It's horrible. It makes me wonder about the real power of love and family.

HOT AIR WILL NOT SAVE THE GULF
by Corina Fiore, Down to Earth Mama blog

Tonight, President Obama gave a speech from the solemn setting of the Oval Office. He supposedly laid out his plan on how we can limit our dependence on foreign oil and how we can help the situation in the Gulf.

What I heard was a lot of hot air.

The president evoked prayer. The president evoked faith. The president evoked our resilience as a nation. The president stated that we are working hard in the Gulf to reclaim the water, stop the well, and clean the beaches.

It was aimed to be a politically safe speech, when there is no such thing in this political climate. No matter what the president says, the right will find fault, pick it to pieces, and play armchair quarterback to express their disgust (cough, cough….. hate) with whatever he chooses to say or do.

So, why play it as you did, Mr. President?

Honestly, I liken this speech, as harsh as it might sound, to President Bush in the wake of 9/11 saying, "Go shopping." This is not what we need. We do not need the eloquence that was meant to appeal to our hopes.

We need a leader.

We need someone to say enough of the talk and red tape. Time for action.

We need someone to tell us that we must make sacrifices and changes in our lives to move us toward getting off oil.

We need someone to tell us that we need to pitch in and help in this crisis and how we can do that.

We need someone with strong words and even stronger actions.

We need someone with a little gnash behind their teeth.

The time for environmental reform and regulation is now. You cannot look at the tragedy in the Gulf, get angry, and then say you will not change your habits. You cannot sit by with your cynicism, tossing up your hands and saying, "Oh well. Nothing is going to change." Because cynicism, while it protects you from the possibility of failure and gives you the ability to say, "I told you so" in the end, is pure laziness. It clears you of all culpability. It limits you, limits the country, entrenches you in a deep ditch where you cannot see above the bank. Aim for the pinnacle. Take a risk, and change your habits. Step up with ideas, instead of tearing down those around you. This is not a crisis to sit back and point fingers. There will be plenty of time for that later. We need more than hot air. We need direction and action.

And there are plenty of us willing to jump in and provide just that.

NOTHING IS GOING TO CHANGE UNTIL WE'RE IN THE ROOM
by Joanne Bamberger, PunditMom blog

White guy, white guy, white guy, white guy, President Obama, Nancy Pelosi, Kathleen Sebelius, *white guy, white guy, white guy who looks like he just ate a sour pickle.*

That's my one-line description of the photo-op image we were presented with of the health-care summit the president called to try one more time in the spirit of harmony and peace to meet with Republicans to fix a very broken health-care system. Or, should I say, it was a genius photo-op event to portray the president as the calm voice of reason while at the same time making the GOP sweat about how this was playing back at home with the constituents.

Aside from whether the summit was more serious policy discussion or brilliant political stagecraft, I have to put the obvious question out there : where were the women? You know, the women who make the bulk of the health-care decisions for their families? The ones who make sure all the insurance paperwork gets submitted? The ones who fight to find health coverage for their families when a few ear infections and a broken bone get a whole family labeled uninsurable because of "pre-existing conditions?"

Sure, there were some staffers in the background and an expert or two wearing skirts. But other than that—not so many women lawmakers, at least compared to the sea of older white guys. Of course, when women only make up about 17 percent of Congress, it is sort of hard to have them represented at the table on anything.

There just aren't enough of us.

I'm sort of surprised that the media noticed at all. Dan Rather commented in a back-handed sort of way:

"If more women were in the room, might the debate have been different? If there were more women in Congress…might our politics be less rancorous and might our elected officials get more accomplished? There's a school of thought that is emerging that suggests the answer is 'yes.'"

A school of thought? An emerging suggestion? The funny thing about that remark is this: no one is screaming at Dan Rather for making such a wild, crazy suggestion that women might run things differently and get us different results! Yet, when Congresswoman Carol Shea-Porter essentially suggested the same thing recently, she was crucified by the far right for being a sexist.

Fortunately, one Congresswoman spoke up at the summit. Congresswoman Louise Slaughter reminded us that when women aren't included, how an entire issue is viewed becomes skewed. And she wasn't just talking about politics—she was also referring to medical studies that are relied upon for treating women but don't include women in the studies.

Unless we're willing to do something about it, though, neither of these phenomena—the absence of women in medical studies and too few women in Congress—will change. I know it's hard to step up to the plate on that one, but surely there are more women out there with the intestinal fortitude to go *"woman a mano"* with the guys.

CHAPTER FOUR

Who's Taking **Care Of** The Kids?

W'e're a country with some serious mother issues.

For proof of that, look no further than media portrayals of modern motherhood to see it's not so "modern" at all. Regardless of what unique situations mothers find themselves in, pop-culture portrayals of motherhood often boil down to the question, "Who's taking care of the kids?" Or rephrasing it to clarify what's really being asked, "Why aren't you taking care of your kids?" In our twenty-first-century world, it would be nice to think we've moved beyond the outdated, 1950s perspective that the role of care-giving naturally lies solely with women.

Television shows like *The New Adventures of Old Christine*, *Desperate Housewives*, and the short-lived *In the Motherhood* all focus on very different portrayals of women as mothers, but all have a similar theme: when women try to combine work and motherhood, they find themselves too frazzled to think straight, become somewhat neurotic, and are treated skeptically if any one of those responsibilities they're juggling happens to fall. Remember Lynette on *Desperate Housewives* sneaking her kids' Ritalin so she could stay awake just to keep up with her family responsibilities? The underlying message isn't subtle—maybe you ladies should give up your day jobs and stay home with the babies.

Programs like these perpetuate the long-running conflict in our society about mothers' roles. Creating shows that encourage us to laugh at women who think they can do it all, while at the same time suggesting that traditional gender roles are a better, easier, and less frenzied way of living, implicitly reinforces how we all think about those long-held societal assumptions about what's acceptable for women. Mothers face the same challenge when they take on the world of politics.

A *CBS/New York Times* news poll[104] taken in the summer of 2007 to assess voters' feelings about Hillary Clinton as a presidential candidate had this as one of its primary questions: *"Generally, do working women make better or worse mothers?"* Really. In 2007. In light of the underlying suggestion that it's still acceptable to ponder whether work and motherhood mix, the results weren't astounding: men are twice as likely to believe that working women aren't good mothers. While technically Clinton was, and is, a "working mother," she hardly fit the mold of someone we envision doing the work/life balance act since her daughter was 27 years old at the time of that poll.

There is still an inherent lack of respect for mothers who dare to step outside what many view as the traditional motherhood mold. That was pretty much proven by countless sexist phrases and euphemisms tossed at Hillary Clinton and Sarah Palin during the 2008 campaign, especially when they were deemed by the male pundits to be talking or acting like mothers. For instance, Jack Cafferty of CNN described Hillary Clinton during the 2008 presidential campaign as a "scolding mother, talking down to a child."[105] Somehow, I suspect Cafferty's mother and the other women in his life might find that as objectionable as most mothers would. Comments such as his raise the question: is that how all mothers are viewed when putting our opinions out there? And even if it is, should we care what the Jack Caffertys of the world have to say?

The questions of whether and how motherhood and elective politics mix were brought to the forefront as never before when John McCain chose Sarah Palin to be his vice-presidential running mate. Once she came on the scene, the struggle over forging young motherhood and politics became a topic everyone wanted to discuss, dissect, and debate, especially as critics insisted on painting the idea with the broad brush of the mommy wars narrative.

News headlines like *"How Good a Mom Can Sarah Palin Be?,"*[106] *"Mom's in the House, With Kids at Home,"*[107] *A New Twist in the Debate on Mothers,*[108] *"Will Palin Bring a Breast Pump on the Campaign Trail,"*[109] and *"The Gentlemom from New York: Sen. Kirsten Gillibrand's Work-Life Balance,"*[110] were proof that questioning the legitimacy of mixing motherhood and politics has become media sport similar to the way in which working motherhood is portrayed in situation comedies. This so-called political analysis suggests that it's fair to question whether mothers really can do it all—and whether we want them to do it all—rather than focusing on their qualifications and the issues they campaign on. Won't a woman be distracted by the serious business of governing if she has to pump breast milk? How will she ever keep tabs on her kids' after-school schedules on the Blackberry? Who's going to be home to cook the mac and cheese, help with homework, and read the bedtime stories?

This 'motherhood and politics don't mix' meme is now firmly entrenched in our political dialogue. Men and women alike are guilty of buying into these long-held assumptions about mothers that have spilled into the realm of public service and political thought. The reality is that women who want to embrace political power, elective or otherwise, will be criticized no matter which side of that maternal line they walk—women like Palin for not being a good mother and mothers like Clinton mocked for being too masculine.[111]

The idea of the good mom paradigm that our society struggles with when it comes to working mothers is now applied to women who dare to be part of the political world. The first children of mothers who were visible in American politics were mostly grown and out of the house, like those of Hillary Clinton and Nancy Pelosi. Or high-profile political women had no children at all—think former senator Elizabeth Dole and current senator Barbara Mikulski. But today we live in an era in which a highly accomplished First Lady like Michelle Obama is forced to shift her public image to that of a traditional stay-at-home mom to be seen as acceptable in the public eye and where a female state governor and vice-presidential candidate is judged not on her record of governing or her ability to analyze political positions, but rather on whether she is neglecting her motherly duties.

And so with the arrival of a new generation of younger political mothers with toddlers and teens still running around the family home, some in the media have been at a loss when it comes to writing about them without reverting to comedic, pop-culture portrayals of motherhood. But there's no joke about what's really happening. When asked about news reports suggesting that Palin was neglecting her family responsibilities by running for vice president, Deborah Tannen, a noted expert on gender and language issues and professor of linguistics at Georgetown University, said these were clear examples of sexism. "What we're dealing with now, there's nothing subtle about it," said Tannen. "We're dealing with the assumption that child-rearing is the job of women and not men."[112]

There's no question that in the last few decades, fatherhood roles have evolved and more fathers are assuming the role of primary caregiver in some families, yet few commentators start discussions on the ability of fathers of young children to mix parental duties and political ambition. Fatherhood has long been viewed differently in our society, with the focus not on care-giving, but on working and providing the means to support a family. Even though it has been decades since the commonly accepted portrait of the family involved a stay-at-home mother and working father who had little involvement in his children's lives, male politicians are rarely described by the media in terms of juggling parenting obligations and professional ambition.

Barack Obama is the father of two young daughters, yet no one questioned his competence for political office or the potential conflict with his fathering duties when he ran for the White House. There were no stories about him during his campaign for the White House with any headlines like *"How Good a Dad Can Barack Obama Be?"* No news reports suggested that Senator John McCain should have abstained from his presidential bid because his youngest daughter was a teen who probably could have used the presence of both parents at home as she navigated her way to high school graduation.

For the most part, political dads get a pass from scrutiny about their mix of parenting and professional obligations in a way mothers almost never do.

Palin's presence gave us plenty of fodder for this mother-as-politician debate, but it wasn't just the media asking the questions about who was going to be tending to Palin's children while she was basking in the political spotlight. Women, too, were divided on the question of whether a mother of young children, including a new special-needs baby, should even toy with the idea of an all-consuming political role. For instance, in her post, *"Will Sarah Palin's Candidacy Set Back Working Mothers?,"* Katherine Lewis, author of the "Working Mothers" column at *About.com*, wrote, ""Sarah Palin either has a screw loose or is a negligent mother. That's the consensus of some of my working mom friends [who are] amazed that she would run for vice president as the mother of [five] children ranging in age from four months to 17 years."

Some commenters at that site thought it would be fabulous to see a vice president wearing a baby carrier aboard Air Force Two (though it's hard to imagine Dick Cheney or Joe Biden wearing a Baby Bjorn!). One reader said that while she disagreed with almost all of Palin's policy views, she felt the media's sexist treatment, judging Palin on her motherhood status, was shameful. On a certain level, we all knew we shouldn't be asking whether Palin could be vice president and manage five children. But since we'd never encountered a candidate like her before, many of us didn't really know how to process this political ubermom phenomenon.

In an "if-you-can't-beat 'em-join-'em" effort, Palin transformed media confusion and curiosity over young mothers entering the world of politics into a new model of motherhood identity politics. Regardless of how we felt about Sarah Palin as a candidate, she was a phenomenon in another way—in addition to being the first woman on a presidential ticket who was also a mother of young children, she also fused her motherhood identity with her political persona on the national stage in a way voters had never seen before. Whether we loved or hated her politics, Palin made us question the assumptions many of us make about who ought to be primarily responsible for child-rearing and whether being a mother to young children is a disqualifier or motivator for elective office.

Palin spoke openly about her belief that her experiences as a mother were definitive qualifications for elective office, a theory that former White House Press Secretary Dee Dee says is a logical one because parents are already seen as leaders in other communities.[123] The experiences of motherhood were part of the motivation for many political up-and-comers. In 2010, former Minnesota State Senator Tarryl Clark, a mother of two college-aged sons, took on Republican Congresswoman Michele Bachmann. Clark's political career blossomed from her work as an attorney who focused on issues involving health care and senior citizens, but she says the relationships she made with other mothers once she had children were also part of her inspiration to run for elective office.[124] Jill Miller Zimon decided that in addition to writing about politics, she was also going to run for an at-large seat on her town council in Ohio, which she won in 2009. And Krystal Ball, with a daughter not even out of diapers, ran for, but lost, a Congressional seat in Virginia's First District in 2010. Invoking parental status as a qualification for political office can have its pitfalls. In 2010, one candidate for Oklahoma governor experienced a profound public backlash when she suggested that she was more qualified than her female opponent because she had children, but her opponent didn't.[125]

While Palin may have been the most scrutinized candidate for having the audacity to believe young motherhood and political ambition could go together like peanut butter and jelly, she certainly wasn't the only woman who drew sexist media critique and backhanded compliments for pursuing her goals.

In an article titled *"The Gentlemom from New York,"* a *Washington Post* writer seemed surprised that Senator Kirsten Gillibrand of New York, a mother of two boys, could manage to fulfill her professional and family roles, as well as finding time to make herself look presentable. Gillibrand says that since being a mother is central to who she is, she will happily accept being called "Senator Mom" [113] or the "gentlemom from New York" as long as people don't assume that her motherhood status limits her political agenda because she, just like many mothers, cares about every issue. As the junior Senator from New York, Gillibrand spends her days focused on issues ranging the full gamut—national security, financial regulatory reform, job creation, terrorism, cyber-security, climate change, updating our country's infrastructure, and farming legislation. Yes, she also advocates for what some would call "mom issues," like healthier and safer food for our children, but that isn't what solely defines her. "As I work in the Senate, I hope to be able to change the perception of what it means to be 'Senator Mom. But in the meantime,

I'm proud of the title."[114]

Maternal sexism in the political world isn't just for the media anymore. There's an ingrained stereotype about mothers that make voters question whether they can even win a race with young children in tow. Pollster and political analyst Celinda Lake's theory is that, rightly or wrongly, voters worry about who's going to be there to take care of the kids if a mother of small children gets elected. It is, she says, one of the clearest double standards left in politics.[115] Stanford University Professor Shelley Correll, who has done extensive research on what has become called the "motherhood penalty" in the workplace, also says it's not a stretch to think that if the mere fact of a woman's motherhood negatively impacts hiring decisions, it could have the same influence on voters' choices.[116]

One Florida congresswoman has experienced that maternal sexism firsthand. The first time Debbie Wasserman Schultz ran for Congress in 2004, she learned that political rivals weren't above playing the 'young moms don't belong in politics" card. Wasserman Schultz's female opponent told supporters that she believed a woman could be a good mom or a good congresswoman, but not both, suggesting that Wasserman Schultz was a bad mother for running for elective office with three small children at home. In an effort to portray the mother of three as a frazzled, disorganized mom who was in over her head by running for Congress, Wasserman Schultz's challenger mocked her for pulling a crayon out of her bag at a candidates' forum, instead of the pen she was rummaging for. Criticizing her mothering ability as a political tactic pushed Wasserman-Schultz to remind the reporter who was writing a story about the episode that it proved nothing about her qualifications and, like any good debate opponent, turned the point around by saying that the only thing it proved was that she was never without a crayon.[117]

This political momism isn't reserved for high profile candidates. Jill Miller Zimon, a City Council member in Pepper Pike, Ohio who also writes the political blog *Writes Like She Talks*, recalls that during her campaign she was frequently asked why she wasn't running for her local school board, since she has three young children. The implication was that because she's the mother of three school-aged children, she should be more focused on running for a child-related political position.[118] Aimee Olivo ran for her school board in Prince George's Country,

Maryland in 2010, and as she was campaigning, was often asked, "Who's taking care of your children?" rather than questions about which issues would be her priority.[119] A voter once told Oregon State Representative Sara Gelser, a mother of four, he couldn't support a candidate with small children because he felt such a person was breaking their first commitment to care for their kids.[120]

The media's insistence on defaulting to overly sexist commentary about political women didn't stop when the 2008 presidential campaign was over. When Palin announced she was resigning as Alaska governor, one cable news anchor wondered aloud if she might be pregnant again. And a subsequent *Vanity Fair* magazine article attempted to dissect the Palin phenomenon by describing her as "the first indisputably fertile female to dare to dance with the big boys," somehow suggesting that her ability to have children had some relevance to a story on her ability to govern. I suspect no one would ever question a male candidate's motivations based on his sperm count or the number of his children.

These assumptions impact all mothers, not just those who choose politics as their vocation. Trying to overcome the stigma and assumptions that mothers are less committed and less competent in a professional setting than those who are childless is difficult for countless women. In some ways, we seem to be going retro in terms of how mothers are viewed when they step out of "traditional" mothers' roles. As writer Susan Getgood reflects at her blog *Snapshot Chronicles* in the post "Has Dooce[121] Become a Modern Day June Cleaver," we continue to struggle with these issues in the twenty-first century because our country's power structure still relies on keeping women in traditional gender roles and romanticizes that supposed ideal. That scenario might be helpful to many working fathers who like to see dinner on the kitchen table at the end of the day, but it's not a positive thing for mothers who are trying to secure more places at the political power table.

No doubt Gillibrand, Wasserman Shultz, Palin, and other mothers have learned from experience how to steel themselves for the inevitable comments about whether one can be a mother to young children and have a high profile life on the American political stage. But when we still get criticized about the crayons in our purses, our ongoing fertility or our ability to manage responsibilities of work and family, we have to ask the same question posed by Leslie Sanchez, a Washington, D.C.-

based political consultant—"Are we as a society really ready to see a strong mother at the political table, especially in the White House?"[122] Insistence on framing stories about women through the lens of traditional motherhood is holding women back—in the workplace, in policy debates, and as news analysts in major media outlets.

As frequently as we are hearing more about the various ways motherhood and politics can combine, for many, having children is a primary reason to avoid running for office. According to long-running research conducted by Jennifer Lawless and Richard Fox, the majority of women even at the highest levels of professional accomplishment are reluctant to run for elective office. One of the main reasons for their hesitance is the burden of still-traditional motherhood obligations.[126] Mothers may become active politically by helping to get out the vote, advocating for causes, or, as we are seeing in the online world, writing opinion essays about issues important to them. But there is still a need to find women ready to take the next step into the influence of holding elective office. For many, however, that idea is still too daunting because of the perceived potential negative impact on their families.[127]

Even highly motivated, successful women fall victim to this phenomenon. Siobhan "Sam" Bennett, president and CEO of the Women's Campaign Forum, is living proof of that. Bennett says that her own motherhood experiences impacted her political views and knows that part of being a mom is influencing our children's environment. A successful businesswoman and PTA president, Bennett had never even considered the possibility of running for office—even though she now believes that her parenting experience definitely qualifies her—until she was courted both by Democratic and Republican leaders in her town to run for mayor. That led to her decision later to run for Congress.[128] She eventually lost both races. But, she says, the idea of running for any office had never crossed her mind and she probably would not have taken that step if she hadn't been encouraged by others.[129]

Notwithstanding the findings of the research from Lawless and Fox, some mothers are starting to see that maybe they could be bold enough to step into the political arena. Teacher and Philadelphia-area mother Corina Fiore may just step up to the plate when slots come open on the school board for her child's school. A teacher, blogger, and mother, Fiore is tired of watching how recent contentious contract negotiations negatively impacted the culture and atmosphere at her child's school. "I wish that teachers, staff, and schools get the credit and honor they deserve for the work that they do each day. I am considering running for our school board because institutions of learning are no place for overinflated egos at our children's expense. I can only hope to make a difference from the inside."[130]

So how do others overcome the natural fear of subjecting themselves and their families to the scrutiny that high-profile political mothers face today? Several organizations are committed to providing the training and support women need to face those challenges, including the She Should Run project at the Women's Campaign Forum;, The White House Project;, Emerge America;, and the recently formed 2012 Project, launched by the Center for American Women and Politics at Rutgers University.

ed For those not quite ready to make that leap, flexing parental leadership muscles online is a first step.. Maybe that will inspire more of us to jump right into the lion's den of our world where extreme politics is viewed as sport. Not only can we use online tools as part of the battleground to express opinions, work for candidates, and advocate on behalf of issues, but we can also work on convincing the naysayers that our motherhood perspectives naturally inform how we view the issues and candidates—and that's a good thing.

WORK-LIFE BALANCE: OUR LADDER IS UP THE WRONG TREE
by Amy Tiemann, MojoMom blog

All the research I have done as "MojoMom" has led me to a conclusion that, as mothers trying to have an integrated life with many facets, we have our sights set on the wrong goal. Our ladder is up the wrong tree in a major way.

I am talking about "work-life balance." This idea is everywhere and has become a watchword for my generation, Gen X, which has put "work-life balance" on the map as our highest ideal as we negotiate with our hard-charging boomer bosses. Although it is usually presented as a positive ideal, "balance" is a trap. I argue that rather than being our highest goal, "balance" accurately describes our current situation that asks families to do it all…on our own. Until we change our thinking on this issue, we are going to be stuck with the same set of unappetizing work-life "choices" that we are faced with now.

Think about it. Who needs balance? Jugglers, tightrope walkers…and moms. Picture the iconic cover of a chick-lit novel, showing a woman struggling to "balance" a briefcase, cell phone, and pacifier. In real life, there would most likely be a dog and stroller involved too, in addition to an actual baby. When we tell women to strive for balance, we're really telling them to keep dancing as fast as they can. We are telling them that they are failing to keep it all together without asking for help.

"Balance" is in fact a telling metaphor for motherhood. Balance is the underappreciated sixth sense in our brains. Our sense of balance is active, dynamic, and takes a constant hum of processing and adjustment to achieve. Yet this vital work barely registers in our conscious mind. We only notice it when our system fails and we are thrown into disequilibrium, left dizzy and unable to function. We couldn't get out of bed to stand up straight and walk, much less work and lead productive lives, without our sense of balance. But when is the last time you thought of your vestibular system, not to mention stopping to thank heavens for the vital job it does?

This is just like the work that mothers provide: unpaid, uncounted, and invisible labor that forms the foundation of family life. If it were counted, women's unpaid household labor would add an estimated one-third to the world's annual economic product, more than $4 trillion.

So if our balancing act is a farce rather than a lofty goal, what should we be aiming for?

Support.

This needs to become our new ideal, our North Star, our guiding metaphor. The motherhood movement should aim for creating a real support network that involves everyone—employers, communities, men and women. We need a team approach to holding up the world, one that recognizes the contributions that all family caregivers make, a system that does not just expect us to make the pieces fit all by ourselves on an individual level. My MojoMom mantra is to "make the invisible work visible and then divide it fairly." We are still at the beginning of that first step, increasing awareness about what mothers and fathers contribute to society, through the sacrificial giving that is required to raise the next generation of children. Support and teamwork need to trickle up from the grassroots to a policy level. We can use this context to explain the motherhood movement to supporters and skeptics alike.

I learned a lesson about support recently. I had ordered a giant beanbag chair called a Foof Cube for our home. My seven-year-old knew a good thing when she saw it. Within a day of its arrival, she had commandeered it for her bed, and she's been sleeping in it every night since then. Kids are great at taking what they need.

I am also ordering another one for myself. In the meantime, I sneak into her room during the school day and sink down into the foam cube to remind myself what support feels like. I am cradled in a snug nest. I let go and nothing falls.

I could get used to this.

THE WORK/MOTHERING COHESIVENESS OF SARAH PALIN
by Tracee Sioux, The Girl Revolution Blog

I just finished *Going Rogue: An American Life* by Sarah Palin, former governor of Alaska and 2008 Republican vice-presidential candidate. I'm going out on a limb and asking readers to put aside their political venom to discuss the *merging* and *blending* of mothering and working.

Take a deep breath. This isn't a post about abortion. It's not a post about Bristol or teen pregnancy. This post doesn't discuss energy, ANWAR, death panels, or the health care bill.

While you read this, if it's humanly possible, put aside your opinions and positions and accept my invitation to look at Sarah Palin in the context of her ability to govern and mother simultaneously.

Sarah Palin is a bad-ass mom.

A quick-run down of what I consider bad-ass mothering: campaigning for mayor and city council door-to-door pulling a wagon full of toddlers, toting her children all over Alaska to campaign for governor, giving birth while governor, breast-feeding a Down Syndrome infant while on the campaign trail running for vice president of the United States of America.

She didn't strike a "balance" between work and motherhood; she cohesively merged her work and motherhood seamlessly. Doing so was to the benefit of her personal fulfillment, her children and her work. She felt a calling for more than motherhood, didn't see a conflict and just DID it. She didn't wait for the historically patriarchal Republican Party's permission. She just did it.

How did she do it? She did what mothers have *always* done throughout the history of mankind: she did what she needed to do and took her kids with her or found someone to watch them.

Her youngest daughter, Piper, one of the primary characters in the book, appears at her mother's side at nearly every pivotal moment in Sarah's political career. Piper might actually be the most empowered girl in America, next to Willow and Bristol. Like other children throughout the history of moms and kids, she tagged along behind or beside her mom. The only difference is that instead of cleaning the house and doing dishes, Piper's mom campaigned, governed a city, then a state, and then ran for vice president. She made speeches, mingled with voters, went door-to-door, and posed for photos ops. She signed laws, dealt with reporters and balanced budgets.

The most beautiful thing about this book and Sarah Palin's perspective is that there is no conflict at all between mothering and governing or mothering and working. She doesn't even waste a single thought on it.

She does not apologize for having children, for bringing children on a campaign, for a baby crying in the background of a phone call, for a child's presence at a press conference or a state dinner, for her child answering a reporter's question, for her children being present at the signing of bills, at the governor's office, or even playing hide and seek in the halls while she hammers out a budget through the night.

Sarah is there; therefore, her children are there. Duh, of course they are.

Think about that for one second. Replay, in your own brain, the number of times you apologize for your children's presence. Too loud in church, disruptive in a meeting, no babysitter for a social function, working from home due to ear infections . . . and on and on. Think of all the guilt you've wasted over it.

She doesn't talk about the stress of it either. Mothering is a pleasure. Governing is a privilege. She loves doing both. She has passion for both roles and finds them fulfilling. Why would she surrender one to an outdated traditional expectation?

She also does not apologize for leaving her children to pursue objectives child-free. She went to a hotel in California, leaving her family for a few weeks for some precious peace and quiet to work on her book. During the presidential race of 2008, she campaigned away from her children on weekdays so they could continue going to school in Alaska. Her husband, Todd; their parents; their extended family; close family friends; her children's friends and parent; and a hired babysitter all pitch in to make sure family life keeps trekking along while she's away. Of course they do. It made me think, *"Wait, why are we making this so hard?"*

She didn't quit when her family life got complicated. It got pretty complicated when she had an unplanned pregnancy while governor of Alaska, then found out the baby boy had Down Syndrome. It was further complicated when, a month after giving birth to Trig, her teenage daughter, Bristol, confessed she was pregnant. Her oldest son had joined the military and gone to Iraq and could die at any moment. Any *normal* family would have a very difficult time adjusting to those circumstances. Before any adjusting could happen, Sarah Palin was asked to run for vice president and hit the campaign trail. And she did it. Come on, I know women who have an emotional breakdown and take a sick day when they get their period every month.

There is a vital difference between her life and most working women's lives: Sarah Palin is the boss.

She has no boss telling her it's inappropriate to bring her kids to work, inappropriate to campaign with a wagon full of toddlers behind her as she talks to voters door-to-door. She has no human resources department counting her sick days and no one telling her she can or can't be home at 3:00 p.m. to greet her kids after school.

There is no one telling her she can't work from her kitchen table when she needs to. No one telling her it's unprofessional to bring children to a budget meeting or a major speech.

Some of us bang our heads against the brick wall of the patriarchal workday establishment asking for maternity leave, paid sick days, and family medical leave. Talking to employers and trying to convince human resource departments of our worthiness as mothers *and* workers. Arguing over legislation, trying to convince politicians to support family medical leave and a flexible workday. And raging against the fact that our available choices all suck (I mean me, here).

Sarah Palin went *around* the brick walls. She just believed such nonsense didn't apply to her. So it didn't. I'm fairly certain it won't apply to her daughters either.

THE SARAH PALIN PROBLEM
by Kari Dahlen, The Karianna Spectrum blog

The media is abuzz about all the different Sarah Palin controversies. Each time I sit down to compile my thoughts on Palin, yet another cringe-worthy accusation, revelation, or admission comes out.

Leave it to the political bloggers, I often think, since it seems impossible to digest the information, much less separate "fact" from "fiction," given that honesty is not the first quality one thinks of when considering a stereotypical politician or staff spin job. But I am in some ways the "target" audience of John McCain's brash VP choice, so I don't want to stay silent.

No, I am not a Republican. No, I am not anti-choice. No, I am not conservative in any of the ways that Palin's supporters are: I don't carry a gun, I don't particularly support the death penalty, and I believe that an abstinence-only education leads to... well, ask Bristol Palin.

Except *don't* ask her, because I don't want Bristol involved. Just like I wish Palin's credentials as a mother or what is between her legs wouldn't be part of the story. Even if I don't believe in Palin's politics, I am drawn into the discussion simply because I am a woman.

I don't want to be lumped together with her just because we share a gender. I don't want to be considered represented by her in any form. McCain may have hoped that women eager to see "one of their own" in a position of power would line up behind him. But instead, I am repulsed.

One of my favorite analogies thus far comes from Wendy Sachs via the *Mommy Track'd* blog:

Instead of finally cracking through the glass ceiling, Palin is likely to just leave more dangerous shards on the ground for women to have to tip-toe through.

Indeed, Palin's "status" as a woman and mother creates an uncomfortable bond-by-association and makes her an unfortunate spokeswoman for high-powered female politicians.

Mentions that she is a mother of five are thrown around to mean "*See, she is a mother. She is just like you,*" but also, "*See what a tough cookie she is. She doesn't let motherhood slow her down.*" For example, she allegedly took two plane flights after her water broke with her son Trig. I cannot imagine putting the health of my baby in danger by flying while in labor, much less without the sterile environment of the amniotic sac.

There are plenty of us out there who *have* been slowed down by motherhood in one fashion or another. It isn't that we are weak; it is that motherhood is difficult. Denying the challenging aspects of being a mother is misleading and insulting.

We shouldn't even be discussing such things, because how Palin chooses to raise her children should be her business. But when personal choices show irresponsibility or deception, then it might signal the capacity to be irresponsible or deceitful on the job. Unfortunately, because she is a mother, these questions of work-family balance come into play.

To some, her juggling act is heroic. To others, it's unrealistic. On one hand, I want to spew forth my opinions on everything that I feel she is doing wrong (*save the national politics for when your children are grown!*) And yet, I recognize that the source of my discomfort is fear that my efforts as a mother will be disregarded. The choices that mothers make surrounding their work-style and parenting-style are already heavily criticized. Much of what I wish for is tolerance of other opinions and flexibility of options. And yet,

I find myself frustrated and fearful that someone like Palin could end up representing me.

I admit that I underestimate the ability of people to separate the different aspects of Sarah Palin into what matters and what doesn't. Because of that, I discuss what *shouldn't* matter, because I want to defend myself in that arena. I want to be respected for my choices, even if others don't make the same decisions.

Not surprisingly, when I learned that Trig has Down Syndrome, I worried. As much as I don't like being considered an "autism mom" and as much as I question my place in the special-needs community at times, I feel a camaraderie amongst those who have had to parent with extra challenges. I worry not about Palin's ability to mother her son, but rather how the media will choose to portray her relationship with her "special needs" son. Specifically, I have concerns about how that portrayal will reflect on other mothers who perhaps don't have the same support system she does. And I certainly don't want her infant son's label to be used as proof that she is "brave" and strong.

I wish the discussion of Sarah Palin could be about her ability to be vice president, and what kind of United States we would have with her in that role or in the role of president. But at this point, it is much, much more.

HOW LONG WILL IT BE UNTIL THE NEXT "VIABLE WOMAN PRESIDENTIAL CANDIDATE?"
by Joanne Bamberger, PunditMom blog

I didn't start out as a Hillary Clinton supporter.

John and Elizabeth Edwards were my presidential couple of choice. In fact, when it became clear, lo' those many years ago, that Hillary was crafting her White House strategy I said to anyone who would listen that she would never be able to be elected—partly because of her Clinton "baggage" and partly because I didn't think this country was ready yet for a woman president.

Uttering those words felt like feminist treason.

But as someone who grew up in a rural community and who has lived in some fairly red areas, I had a bad feeling in my gut that

America wasn't ready.

It looks like I was right.

Many have argued that such a notion is nonsense, After all, plenty of other countries have had women leaders, so surely it was time for the U.S. to join those ranks.

But America lags in so many things that benefit women—reproductive rights, numbers of women involved in government (we're behind plenty of countries, including the United Arab Emirates and Argentina, to name just two), and maternity leave benefits—that I doubted whether we as Americans possessed the basic amount of respect toward women needed to put one in charge of the whole country. If lawmakers won't acknowledge women's value to our economy or that certain rights should be permitted under the law, how can we conceive of one pulling up with the moving van to 1600 Pennsylvania Avenue?

When the Supreme Court pronounces that women are incapable of making decisions about their own reproductive rights, saying that their abortion decision in *Gonzalez v. Carhart* was for "[women's] own good," what hope is there that our country can imagine someone who wears skirts (or pantsuits) making decisions about everyone?

Sure, we've come a moderate way, baby, but not far enough to take that last step.

I wanted to be wrong. I really did. So when John Edwards dropped out of the race, I decided to support Hillary over Obama, in large part, because her health-care plan was essentially the same as Edwards'—real coverage for everyone—whereas Barack Obama's is not. Yes, it's *way* better than what the Republicans want, but it's still not health care for everyone.

I also became the teensiest bit excited about the possibility of being able to show my daughter that girls really could be and do anything, and thought it would be special to make plans with her to watch as Hillary took the oath of office as the first woman president of the United States.

Clinton is in campaign shut-down mode, and I'm a bit depressed. Not because I thought she was the best candidate to be our next president, but because of what it says about our country, its views on women and how much longer that road is than I had thought.

We're not ready for a woman president. So if not now, when?

Given the treatment Hillary has received as a candidate, I fear it will be a long time before another woman is ready to subject herself—and her family—to the meat grinder of American presidential politics.

ZIMON WINS COUNCIL SEAT
by Jill Miller Zimon, Writes Like She Talks blog

Not too long ago, I wrote about my fantasy of how I would break the news to my family and tell them that I wanted to run for public office.

The vision went like this: I would deploy projectors, statistics, voter registration information, graphic displays and fundraising schemes to persuade them that they could give up Mom for a few months and she could pursue serving the common good of the bigger whole—even if it's "just" a 6,000-person bigger whole.

My youngest child busted up that plan but good after he noticed a book on my night table called, *How to Win a Local Election.* Having just completed a civics lesson on local government a couple of months earlier, he put two and two together and nailed me before I could make the sell. Luckily, my family has played along nicely with the basis for that fantasy—my dream of running for office—so I probably was, once again, over-preparing to oversell.

Now, as adults and especially as parents, we talk a lot about being good role models, walking the walk and putting our money where our mouths are. In this case, however, many thanks go to my son for proving the relevance of what would otherwise be just clichés. Barely a month ago, and now in the next grade, my son who caught me in the act of seeking elected office decided that he would run for office.

We have a daily school-day routine when my kids come home that involves them giving me their lunch bags and all "parent" papers. One day this fall, during that chore, my son's blank form for a student council candidate's speech wafted out of his trapper. As I picked it up and read it simultaneously, I asked him about it.

"So are you thinking of running this year?" I asked.

"I am, but I don't want you to read what I write." I could tell he was firm in this assertion because he swiped the document from my hand and marched up to his bedroom, folding the paper in half and hiding it away for a week.

Eventually, my son did let me read his stump speech, but not until the morning that he would be giving his presentation. By then, nothing I could say to him would impact his campaign plan. So I just wished him luck and smiled as he left for school.

I had to pick him up that day because he had a doctor's appointment. As I parallel-played at home all day working on my campaign, I wondered to myself how it had gone for him.

As soon as he opened the car door and slung his backpack inside, I assumed that he would burst out with, "I won!" or slump over with a, "Well, there's always next year."

Instead, all I got was a "did you bring me a snack to have in the car on the way to the doctor's office?"

Huh?

"Hey! How about the student council elections? How did it *goooooo*?" Look, if I'm not getting closure on my race for what feels like an eternity, the least I can get is satisfaction from my son's experience.

"Oh, yeah. I won." He was enthusiastic, sincerely, but exclamation marks just would not do it justice.

As it turned out, he faced 10 competitors, all of whom read their prepared statements to the classroom. Then they voted. My son said that according to his teacher, he won more than half the votes in the class, which, in a race with a total of 11 candidates and 23 students, sounds like a pure landslide.

This story is cute all on its own, right? Lots of kids see the movie *Election* and watch the zeal of actress Reese Witherspoon's character as she sets out to get elected as her high-school class president.

Here's the final hanging chad to count on why we should practice what we preach: My son ran for student council even though he had lost in the previous year. Now that made this mother proud.

AT THIS RATE, SOON WE'LL ALL BE TRACY FLICK
by Joanne Bamberger, PunditMom blog

Remember Tracy Flick from the movie *Election?* The over-achieving, uber-ambitious, won't-let-anything-get-in-my-way gal running for class president? If she didn't before, U.S. Senator Kirsten Gillibrand is now very familiar with Tracy, who some are saying is Gillibrand's alter ego.

If Tracy Flick was a real person she'd now be 28—old enough to have run and won a seat in Congress (you *KNOW* she would have). But she would *NOT* be happy that yet another, successful, high-profile woman politician is getting compared with Tracy's less attractive characteristics.

In the span of less than a year, Gillibrand is the third major woman candidate to endure this ever-more-common comparison. The media had a field day comparing Hillary Clinton to a ruthless Tracy. Then the media voices chimed in with the same for Sarah Palin, describing her as "ferocious overachiever Tracy." Now, Gillibrand is the latest to be tagged with the Tracy Flick persona.

Really? I could have sworn we were out of high school with the whole name-calling thing, but apparently I was mistaken.

In comparing Gillibrand to the fictional Flick, *New York Times* columnist Maureen Dowd described her as "opportunistic and sharp-elbowed." A man with those same qualities? He'd be painted as "knowing how to seize the moment with a take no prisoners approach." Dowd wrote, "Fellow Democrats were warning Harry Reid…that he was going to have his hands full with the new senator because she's 'a pain.'" A man wouldn't be called a pain; he'd be called persistent.

But there's a bigger issue than just semantics. As we allow ourselves to be painted in these terms without objecting, we set the stage for a play we don't want our daughters cast in. If we let it go on, we allow a new common wisdom to be born.

The first comparison to Tracy Flick was new. The second time could be called a coincidence. After three times, it's accepted shorthand for devious, calculating, and bitchy. Is that how we really want the women and girls we're encouraging to run for office to be described? One of these days, one of them will be President of the United States and I don't want to hear anyone comparing her to Flick in that way.

I'm not the only one thinking along these lines. *The New Agenda* blog termed it the "SOB"-ing of women in politics, where the media have "simplified, objectified, and bimbo/bitchified" them.

In 2008, it became acceptable political commentary to mock women politicians as divas, ditzes, bitches, and bimbos. If it doesn't change, why would any of our daughters ever think about becoming our next generation of leaders? They won't.

Granted, I'm guilty of it, too. I compared Palin to Tracy Flick during the campaign. Sometimes, comparisons are valid. But when it's the same one for every XX-er who comes on the political scene, it ceases to be fair in individual instances and starts to portray political women only in the extreme, fictional, cartoony world of Tracy Flick.

To those who see only her faults, let's not forget there was a good side to Tracy Flick. She saw the system for what it was and took it on anyway in hopes of accomplishing something good. Tracy realized before Tina Fey ever said it, that *"bitches get things done."*

I like that in a girl. Maybe the next Tracy Flick comparison can be to that quality.

THE PALIN PENUMBRA
by Katherine Reynolds Lewis, CurrentMom.com

I have a problem with Sarah Palin.

When the Alaska governor emerged as the Republican party's first female vice-presidential nominee, I wanted to stand up and cheer. Finally, a mother of young children in the running for one of the highest offices in the land! But the more I learned about Palin—and the more public appearances she made—the more my rear end remained fixed to the chair and my brow furrowed in puzzlement. Given the response from my readers at About.com whenever I write about Palin, I'm not alone in having a powerful reaction to this polarizing figure in U.S. politics.

My problem with Palin begins with the judgmental feeling that rises in my gut when I ponder some of the choices she's made in her life. For instance, if I were giving a speech while pregnant with a baby with Down syndrome, and my water broke, I would've headed straight to the hospital. I definitely wouldn't have flown from Texas to Alaska, given birth and then returned to work three days later. If my unmarried, teen daughter turned up pregnant, I would've immediately taken her out of the national spotlight and encouraged her to consider better options for her unborn baby than being raised by a single, teen mom.

Almost as soon as I write these words, I start to cringe. I know there are plenty of people who look at my own life choices and feel that same sense of righteous judgment. How could she put a six-month-old baby in daycare? What about that week-long vacation getaway with her husband when her toddler was barely two? And who would leave two children under six alone with Dad for two weeks while Mom goes to Asia for her grandmother's funeral? (Answer: me.)

So when I judge Palin and presume to know what's best for her family, I leave the door open for other people to do the same to me. No outsider can fully see into a family or a relationship and understand it as well as the participants. How can we, complete strangers, decide what's best for Sarah Palin and her family? Women have stayed second-class citizens in the workplace for so long in part because employers, supervisors and policy makers assume that we will eventually leave the labor force or scale back our ambitions due to motherhood. Wouldn't it be a gift to our children if we could suspend judgment and work toward a world where adult men and women make their life and work decisions based on what's in their hearts—not out of lack of options, economic necessity or societal pressure?

Politically, I consider myself an Independent who believes in personal and fiscal responsibility, social justice and equal rights regardless of gender, sexual orientation, race or disability. Some of Palin's rhetoric is appealing to me on the surface—but she fails to back it up with substance. That brings me to the second part of my problem with Palin. For how she portrays herself as a straight shooter who cuts through the jargon, I don't ever believe that she understands the details of the policies she claims to support. I'm troubled by the thought that she climbed rapidly to the top ranks of U.S. politics because of her physical appearance and not her brain.

But even bringing up Palin's pretty face and trim figure triggers accusations of sexism. Am I failing to take a female politician seriously because she's attractive? Am I jealous? Palin's sex appeal has undoubtedly advanced her career—but President Barack Obama's appearances in a bathing suit also drew flattering media attention. In fact, haven't we all used our appearance and sexual charisma to our own benefit, whether professionally or in negotiating a better price with the car salesman?

As a feminist, I want powerful women in public life to be permitted to be sexual and attractive. I want my daughters to have role models who achieve personal and family goals, as well as their career goals, without having to choose between the two realms. I want my children to believe they can become mothers without sacrificing their ambition. I just wish they had a better role model than Sarah Palin.

TEN THINGS I FREAKING LOVE ABOUT SARAH PALIN
by Tracee Sioux, The Girl Revolution blog

1. She reminds me of my mother.
2. She kind of reminds me of my mother-in-law.
3. She reminds me of myself actually.
4. She's ballsy. She stood up to all the *mean girls* who trashed her and the *perverts* who made *pornography* of her and the *media* who mocked her. She did it with grace, complete sentences (unlike our current resident moron) and with *HUMOR* and a big wide smile on her face.
5. She refuses to stay in the box society made for her. In fact, she pretends there is no box.
6. She believes in God and she believes God has a plan for HER. So do I.
7. Seriously, she breast fed her baby in the limo and green rooms before those speeches. Let me repeat—she breast fed her baby

on the campaign trail. That's cool. That's freaking amazing.

8. She realized kids are portable and brought them with her to campaign instead of refusing a once-in-a-lifetime opportunity to pursue her dreams "because she has kids."

9. She's ambitious.

10. She's beautiful AND smart. Yes, world, women can be pretty AND smart. We don't have to pick one.

In fact, the ONLY thing I don't like about Sarah Palin is her politics *this year.* In eight years she'll be more mature and more experienced and qualified enough if she can keep her nose clean in Alaska.

Barack Obama is the LAST man I will vote for before a woman serves as president of the United States. So some Democratic women better step up to the plate and groom themselves for a solid run in eight years. Hear that EMILY's List and The White House Project? It's Sarah Palin if you can't train a female superstar to step up to the plate and win in eight years. I'll even send you money and help you groom her, but I'm not voting for another pro-woman MAN.

I WILL vote for Sarah Palin *in spite of her politics* to break the glass ceiling on 2016.

In fact, the way I figure it—if Barack Obama does what he says he's going to do, then I will be satisfied with my equal pay, universal healthcare, family medical leave insurance, and solid standing in the Supreme Court, and an economy healed by using cash to pay as we go.

The Republican Party will have reinvented itself, brought in some young blood like Sarah Palin and kicked out the crazies who are against birth control, or I'll be menopausal so it won't be that important to me.

Obama will have healed the racial divide and sexism will be the final social frontier (OK, there will still be homophobia, but it, too, will be less pronounced in eight years) and I'm sorry people, I don't give a crap how much you personally hate her, feel offended by her, feel jealous of her, feel defensive by her outward morality—I NEED to see a woman in the highest office of that land.

More importantly *MEN* need to see it so we can earn their

damned respect. My children need to see it, both my son and my daughter. If that woman is Sarah Palin, well, she'll be highly entertaining to watch for eight years. We might learn a few useful tricks from her about how to have it all. I'll be watching her.

SARAH PALIN, AMERICA'S NEXT TOP UBER-MOM?
by Joanne Bamberger, PunditMom blog

Sarah Palin is a mother. So am I. That's where our similarities end.

Since I'm a pretty progressive Democrat and she's, um, not, there aren't a lot of things we agree on politically. We don't have a lot in common in how our motherhood experiences look, either.

I don't have five kids and I'm not a governor (though I was a PTA mom, so maybe I'm headed in that direction!). But more importantly, in the discussion about working mothers in America there's this—I don't have the support network or work situation that Palin does that has given her the luxury to bring home the caribou bacon and fry it up in a pan. So whether you're a Democrat, a Republican or something else entirely, I have to wonder whether it's fair to hold Sarah Palin up as the new standard of working motherhood?

I have only one daughter at home, and I find it almost impossible at times to juggle her schedule, household obligations (please don't stop by my house unannounced if you know me) and, oh yeah, work. Palin is, to say the least, lucky. She has a bevy of family and friends who have taken over for her when she can't take the kids to the office or be home for their school and social obligations.

I don't have that. Zippo. Nada. And there are plenty of working parents who don't either. Nor do they even have decent, affordable child care to try to make the whole crazy puzzle work.

There's a whole host of reasons our personal parenting safety net is non-existent, including the fact that we don't live close to many family members. I suspect there are many families in the same situation, ones who would give anything if a mom, sister, cousin or aunt lived close by to help out.

So will this uber-mom portrait that has been painted of Palin force the rest of us to don the cape and become super-moms ourselves?

At the blog Conversation Starter,[131] Christina Bielaszka-DuVernay comments that whether we can be uber-moms is a function of life circumstances:

> Men and women are different, and their parenthood experiences in the early months or years of a child's life are different. I was hired [in my current job] when I was eight months pregnant. Because this hire happened in April and my husband's teaching schedule allowed him to be a full-time parent in the summer months, I returned to my very new job when my first child was only eight weeks old. My company's lactation rooms allowed me to continue breast-feeding, but nothing anyone could do—not my employer, not my spouse—could alleviate the wrenching exhaustion of working an 8-to-6 schedule when night after night. I slept in two-hour shifts because I was nursing. By my second week back, I was, quite literally, walking into walls.

I worry that, regardless of what happens to Palin in November, having her in the spotlight has put an unwanted spin on what successful, modern working motherhood should look like. While there's much to admire in the punching-through-the-maternal-wall perspective, if we start to raise the bar on what motherhood should look like, as described by Kathy G. at The G Spot blog,[132] then what happens?

> A prime example is an excellent article by Katherine Marsh in the New Republic. Marsh analyzes how Palin's image as an [Ayn] Rand-ian superwoman reinforces right-wing tropes that government help for working women, such as paid leave and publicly provided child care, is not necessary. 'Stop whining—I did it on my own, and so can you!' is basically the message Palin delivers, where issues of sexism and work/family balance are concerned. But unlike Palin, few of the rest of us are lucky enough to have a well-paying job, a stay-at-home husband, and a strong, supportive network of relatives who are happy to pitch in where child care duties are concerned.

I can't do it all on my own without the circle of support that Palin has, but somehow I muddle through with some things, OK many things, inevitably falling through the cracks.

No neat home. Stacks of laundry and paperwork everywhere. Homework that has to be finished, social obligations (not big ones, just little things like remembering birthdays), and food in the house. These are the things I struggle with because in my world, there is no village there to chip in to allow me to pursue the career I love with abandon.

That's OK with me—I love my crazy, messy life and wouldn't give up the time I get with my daughter for anything. I just don't want the rest of the world to expect me to live up to the Sarah Palin model of motherhood since it's getting applause from so many.

For most of us, real life just doesn't work that way.

STANDING UP FOR WORKING MOTHERS, INCLUDING SARAH PALIN
by Robyn Roark, Who's the Boss? blog

Last Saturday night, I attended a family function with my very conservative, very Republican extended family. I often make jokes about how I love them despite this fatal character flaw. And they often make similar jokes about me. The truth is, we simply don't agree on nearly every aspect of politics and on many other issues. We probably won't ever agree. Since they can't change my mind and I can't change theirs, politics rarely comes up.

When the election came up during a conversation on the economy, I kept my mouth shut. I know my family will vote for McCain-Palin. My family knows I will vote for Obama-Biden. I'm glad that I live in a blue state where I worry a little less about my family's vote. I kept myself out of the conversation until the only other liberal in my family made a comment about whether or not Sarah Palin can handle the job with her young family. I couldn't stay silent any longer.

Can we stop judging Palin for being a working mother? Really, the fact that she has children, even young children, has nothing to do with anything. I know that she herself has brought up her working mother status in numerous speeches. I think that being a working mother is nothing to be ashamed of. I'm glad that she has brought to the surface the juggling act that all working parents face each and every day.

Yes, I can relate to Sarah Palin. We are both working mothers. She works in the old-boys club of government. I work in the old-boys club of corporate America. I am glad that a woman is still in this race. For the first time (historians, please correct me if I am wrong), we have a woman running for a national executive office who still has babies and toddlers underfoot. Being a working mom, I think that is exciting and validating.

I have fought against maternal profiling in the workplace. I've heard story after story of women being passed up for promotions, on high-profile accounts, on assignments that require travel just because they are mothers. I've seen women be perceived as being slackers, and I've heard that singletons refer to us as "breeders" in the workplace. I've been asked to "talk to my husband" before I book my travel arrangements and grilled on my child-care arrangements. I've had people assume that I don't want to go to the after-hours office party because I'd rather be with my family.

I am sick of people questioning whether or not she can do the job with a special-needs child. I am sick of people assuming she won't have any time for her children if she makes it into the White House.

Let Sarah Palin decide what is right for her family. And let the people of America decide what is best for America. I obviously won't be voting for Palin. My decision is based on the issues and the candidates' the platform. It has nothing to do with her status as a working mother.

THE DISNEY EMPIRE AND THE ALIENATION OF HILLARY CLINTON
by Jen, MOMocrats blog

From the time we were young, boys and girls alike are infused with fairy tales. As we all know, the premise of fairy tales revolves around good versus evil/victory over persecution, and generally portrayed through a victim/heroine/beautiful girl who usually is saved by a hero/prince after fighting some sort of battle against a villain/ evil-doer/often a wicked stepmother/witch/and in one case a weird female sea creature.

And intentional or not, this shit is keeping Hillary Clinton down.

At the end of the day, our country has proved itself more ready to elect a man of color over a woman, and whether you like Hillary or not it poses the question: is misogyny embedded more deeply in our country's foundation than racism? The subtle and not-so-subtle mistrust, anger, sexualization, and underestimation of women in our society is indisputable, and mainstream media does little to quell the flames with its advertising and programming and yes, its political coverage.

Portraying Hillary as manly, as emotional, as a bitch are all ways her gender is subtly and not so subtly brought into the equation. Online forums are no better. One of the popular political groups on Facebook is called *Hillary Clinton: Stop Running For President and Make Me a Sandwich.* We've found all sorts of ways to work 'bitch' into a statement about Hillary, both from Tina Fey's positive and brilliantly pointed *Bitch is the New Black* to all of the derogatory statements about *why folks can't vote for her, she's too much of a bitch.* Now if Obama was getting equal time for being called a "dick" that would be one thing, but have you heard anyone say "dick" is the new Black? Bringing dick Back? I'm a dick and Proud?

Oh wait. Dick's been in charge all along.

Before you call me a man-hater (which I am not) and a Hillary supporter, (which I am still undecided), or worse, and accuse me of making a big deal out of nothing because this isn't about all women, folks just don't like HER, I ask you simply: if Cinderella's nemesis was a wicked stepfather and she ended up selling the glass slipper on eBay to pay for a round-the-world trip with a couple of girlfriends, would we be in this predicament today? And are we willing to keep showing our children that this way of defining women is acceptable?

And will we ever be able to see a woman as commander in chief?

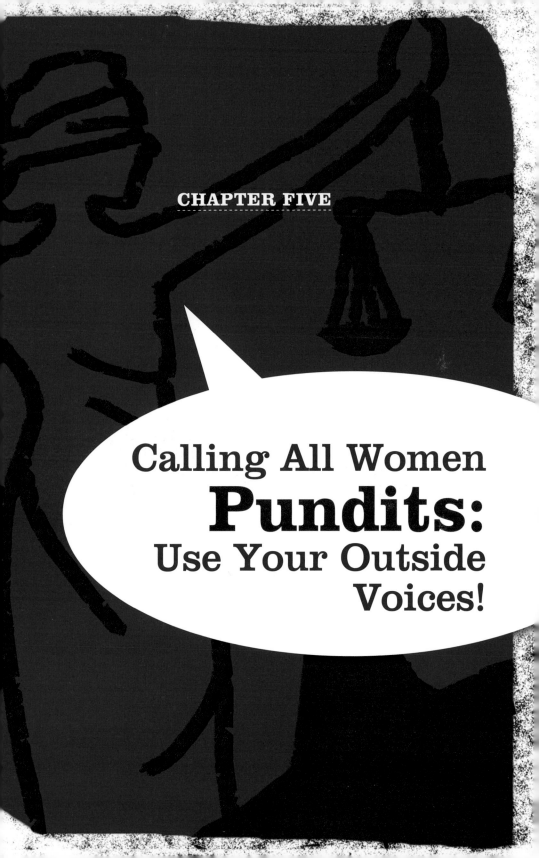

CHAPTER FIVE

Calling All Women
Pundits:
Use Your Outside
Voices!

In the spring of 2010, an article that appeared in the inside-the-D.C.-beltway publication *Politico* spurred a lively conversation among women online. The piece entitled "New Pundits: Prodigies or Pipsqueaks"[133] focused on the increasing influence of 20- and 30-something political pundits in major news outlets. While there's nothing like fresh blood in the world of commentary to give us all new and different perspectives on the world, the story reflected an unspoken reality that something isn't all that fresh about these "pipsqueaks." Like the vast majority of other political analysts, these highlighted newcomers are men. Nary a mention in the article of the increasing presence of women pundits or the influence they have with their unique perspectives—old or young, liberal or conservative, white, black, green or blue. Nada.

Old-school pundit and *Newsweek* journalist

Howard Fineman weighed in on these young turks of commentary for the article, saying that their presence in the world of punditry reflects a paradigm shift in political analysis. I'm not sure what paradigm that would be since the overwhelming majority of pundits for decades have been men. To suggest that adding more testosterone to the already predominantly male world of political punditry amounts to any kind of paradigm shift reflects a blindness to the importance of true diversity in political conversation and influence.

Challenges and reaction to the *Politico* article came quickly. Stories like "Where are the Women Pundits?"[134] and "What About the Next Great Female Pundit?"[135] lamented, in essence, "what's a girl gotta do to get some mainstream media attention around here?" They highlighted the fact that increasing numbers of women are flexing their opinion writing muscles, but with much less recognition than the guys. Women are embracing their inner pundits like never before, with their commentary appearing in many online spaces, but we are still seriously underrepresented in high-profile venues that influence policymakers; even when we are there, we're largely ignored by the power players.

Sure, we have a handful political lady kahunas who get a lot of the spotlight—Arianna Huffington of *The Huffington Post*, Joan Walsh of *Salon.com*, Ann Coulter, and Michelle Malkin, just to name a few. Some spaces dedicated to women's online commentary were created, like *Salon's* Broadsheet, *Slate's* The XX Factor, and *Politics Daily's* Woman Up. But in the short time since those sites went up creation, two are now defunct, with only Slate's XX Factor remaining. So by comparison, women in general, and mothers in particular, still rank pretty low on the general punditry food chain and their major media presence doesn't come anywhere close to that of men.

When looking for "fresh" voices, cable news shows like MSNBC's *Morning Joe* and *Hardball* still tap more men—such as former Congressman-turned-Wall-Street-investment banker Harold Ford and, before he was given his own show on CNN, disgraced former New York Governor Eliot Spitzer—than women. And even at sites that are owned and run by women like *The Huffington Post* and *The Daily Beast*, men are still in the extreme majority of their political writers.[136] For some reason, there's a blind spot when it comes to featuring the growing numbers of women political analysts, with few media leaders reaching out to find and promote the voices of women and mothers.

It isn't that far a leap to suggest that a "maternal wall" effect that many academics have found to exist in the workplace—where, once they become mothers, women are perceived to be less competent and are given fewer professional opportunities—is also present in the world of political commentary. While our society generally views it as acceptable for women and mothers to talk about "mom issues"—work/life balance, child care, and the like—mothers aren't viewed as having the gravitas to speak or write about more serious topics, such as nuclear treaties, economic policy or war.[137]

Some in the media claim there are few women political pundits because women don't want to dive into the political shark tank.[138] Others just don't think to look beyond the mostly male experts they already know. One theory has it that since men still largely decide who is featured in news stories and political conversations in the media, they naturally default to those with whom they feel comfortable: other men. That theory is borne out in a 2010 study by *National Public Radio*,[139] which found a serious lack of expert women's voices in their own reporting.

Even then, the study was challenged by one *NPR* anchor, who suggested that the report was "unsatisfying" and speculated that perhaps the skew toward men as commentators and expert sources was due to "societal factors." But one male reporter interviewed for the study said that it had just never occurred to him to make a point of including a woman source in every piece he filed. When he was required to do that by his employer, he initially resisted, unsure of how that extra work would create a better quality news story. However, as he told the NPR ombudsman who conducted the study, he soon discovered that the inclusion of women offered fresh viewpoints he hadn't previously considered.

Clearly, the uphill battle for women pundits is still a steep one.

The definition of a pundit is an expert—one who analyzes events in the media and politics through a particular life lens and someone with plenty of well-informed opinions. How can one become an expert, a pundit, without some real time in the trenches of life? That's why mothers are the next new source of pundits—there's nothing they know more about than real life.

Mothers deal with the full spectrum of pundit-worthy topics in their lives every day. They live and breathe economic policy since they make approximately 80 percent of all major spending decisions in house-holds.[140] Moms understand the need for paid sick-leave policy as they weigh keeping their sick children home from school against taking time off from work—and losing pay because of it. It shouldn't be a great leap of logic to view mothers as valued political commentators.

Commentary and punditry from typical life experiences is power-ful, especially when it transforms abstract policies into analysis that everyone can relate to. It might even turn our partisan echo chambers into actual conversations. Good opinion writing can't be done without perspective, but unfortunately, many media outlets today have more of a taste for over-generalized, flame-throwing faux-commentary than for reasoned, pithy analysis that embraces real-life experience. Wouldn't it be more constructive to offer analysis that actually helps voters and law-makers alike understand the issues we all face?

Tapping into women's personal experiences could create brilliant new pundits. Our personal lives—our kids, our homes, our friends and our communities—motivate us. And much of women's online writing is personal and embraces the power of narrative storytelling, so why not use that same approach when we get into the meat of politics?

Here's part of the problem: many women don't view themselves as experts and are hesitant to weigh in with opinions based on their per-sonal experiences. One remedy for that might be to embrace our inner third-graders! As a mother, I know that eight- and nine-year-old girls still believe they can accomplish anything and haven't yet developed a fear that their ideas will be dismissed simply because of their gender. An in-spiring example of this fearlessness comes from Lisa Maatz, the director of public policy and government relations for the American Association of University Women. In her essay entitled 'The Great Grammar School Bathroom Door Revolt' in the book *Secrets of Powerful Women*,[141] Maatz recounts how her political involvement all started over a door.

When she was an eight-year-old elementary school girl, she thought it was unfair that the boys' bathroom had doors on the stalls, but those in the girls' bathroom didn't. She and her friends had to shield each other for a little privacy if they needed to use the bathroom during the school day. Maatz remembers she was confident that if she politely asked the principal to give the girls bathroom doors, that he'd get it done. She was crushed when all she got was a dismissive pat on the head, telling her not to worry about such things. Instead of chalking it up to the world of grown-ups versus children and moving on to the next thing, Maatz started a petition, got all the girls in her school to sign it, and at the end of the week, presented it to the principal, saying simply but directly, "I'm not the only one who wants doors." The principal was dumbfounded by the effort, but Maatz got her doors. If more of us could channel those semi-activist moments many of us probably had as children and embrace our fearless inner third-grader, we could make a little more noise and get a lot more done.

But there is a chance that the state of the world today will help speed things up in the realm of mothers' political voices. In stretching our political muscles, it's important to step back and look at the possibility that our world may be transforming into a place where women's values trump the old way of doing things, making more room for mothers' voices in the world of pundits. Claire Shipman, ABC News journalist and co-author of the book *Womenomics: Write Your Own Rules for Success*, predicts that our post-recession period may help with that. She theorizes that as men take a lot of the heat for the world's problems, like the near meltdown of the global economy in 2008, society's values will become more "feminized," thus opening the door for women's increased involvement as thought leaders.

But rather than wait, some activists are actively recruiting and training women to secure more places at the punditry table. In 2008, Catherine Orenstein, author of *Little Red Riding Hood Uncloaked: Sex, Morality and the Evolution of a Fairy Tale,* created a program called The Op-Ed Project, an initiative to expand the pool of women's voices in the world of opinion writers. According to her research, 85 percent of the stories we read on the opinion pages and hear on news talk shows are told by what the site calls "white privileged men."[142] The same is true in other influential venues—men comprise 87 percent of Wikipedia contributors, 85 percent of Hollywood producers and 83 percent of Congress.[143]

Thanks to Orenstein's training sessions and encouragement, the numbers of women appearing on the op-ed pages are increasing. But they are still quite low compared to men. In an attempt to track the evolution of women experts and opinion makers and whether we are making any headway, The Op-ed Project's blog called *The Byline* project is tracking statistics for opinion pieces. In late November 2010,[144] the numbers, sadly, looked like this:

	NYT	WaPo	WSJ	HuffPo	Salon	Daily Beast
% by women	11	23	22	23	18	36
% by men	89	77	78	77	82	64

Though the percentages fluctuate depending on the week or month, those are some daunting numbers, especially when viewed along with the similarly small numbers of women analysts included on the Sunday morning news talk shows.[145]

None of us is going anywhere politically, whether as pundits or elected officials, unless and until we decide to take the journey together. Orenstein clearly knows that, since the premise of The Op-Ed Project is to nurture the idea of collective women's voices in major opinion forums. Other groups and organizations have followed suit. The Women's Media Center has created a program called Progressive Women's Voices to train more women for media appearances as experts, while Smart Girl Summit has become an annual event to help cultivate the voices of politically conservative women.

The idea of women taking the journey together to create more influence for our ideas and opinions is a basic one. To use an old analogy, women are infamous for going to the ladies' room together, so as former White House Press Secretary Dee Dee Myers has joked, why not approach political agendas in the same way and do it together? U.S. Senator Kirsten Gillibrand, editor-in-chief of *More Magazine* Lesley Jane Seymour, political consultant Leslie Sanchez, and many others agree—if we're ever going to move forward politically, we've got to do it together. Regardless of political affiliation, women as a whole agree on about 80 percent of major issues. If we can promote each other in the way that The Op-Ed Project has started to do, it won't be long before our voices are heard as clearly and loudly as those of men. Social media tools and online communities can strengthen those efforts.

In her book *On Becoming Fearless*, Arianna Huffington implored women to find their "inner force" to speak out on important issues. I believe that's exactly what's happening online, but people need to know where to look for it. When we use our personal experiences and narratives, we connect with each other and move our collective political agendas forward.

That's how we're all going to become Mothers of Intention, by stepping out of our safety zone and using the things that have made us who we are to change the political world in the ways we want.

Many women have begun stepping into the world of fearlessness by writing about their views and opinions in a variety of online spaces. They are writing with conviction and humor, sharing how their life experiences color their perceptions of our political world, which is still mostly run by, reported on and analyzed by men. But that's changing.

The new world of online media, social media, blogs, and virtual communities has brought like-minded women closer together than ever before. As a result, the political voices of millions of women and mothers are gaining volume and prominence that was unheard of just a few years ago. Sure, we still have a long way to go before the political establishment sees us as the new paradigm, but there will come a point when our impact and influence can't be denied anymore.

BE A REAL PROGRESSIVE: TAKE A TEA PARTIER TO LUNCH
by Lorelei Kelly, Huffington Post blog

Ronald Reagan must be smiling. A massive snowstorm just closed down the federal government and disproved global warming. (joke!). But as I sit here with the snow drifting 12 feet off the ground, covering my windows—eating 70-percent cacao chocolate bars (cupboards bare!)—what amazes me is the silence. Snow has rendered Washington, D.C. speechless. Now *that* takes a freak of nature.

How might we use this frozen pause? Would it be possible to take the next 48 hours while we East Coaster organizing types are sitting around online, to think about how to start again?

I've been reading the back and forth about whose fault it is—our collective hangover after getting drunk on Hope and Change. But our lack of perceived progress can't be blamed on the president or on the Tea Party movement. It goes deeper than that. Part of the problem is a worldview on the left that has so many moving parts, it is incoherent. When I worked on Capitol Hill, I saw this as one after another liberal group came to advocate for their narrow issue without tying it into a larger idea. A bigger problem to solve is how to anchor all these parts—to organize their public purpose and thereby influence government. Congress is not doing its civic job: to mediate between the local and the national for the good of the whole. And private interests—both corporate and ideological—have filled the gap with their constant, helpful presence. (It's not just about money, it's about timing, relationships, and bringing useful information into the room). And even though they are making strides, funders on the left still seem willing to fund opposition more than governing. In other words, they'll get people in the street, but not in the room.

Maybe it shouldn't be a surprise. The two main themes of government over the past four decades have been Reagan's sunny destruction and the Boomers' anti-authority shouting. These two negative beams have now crashed and left a vacuum right where government—by the people—should be. Who is for the government these days? One great example is how the left and right blend into one when discussing "special interests." Anyone with a healthy sense of public purpose knows that some interests ARE special. Like children and peace. Others are commercial interests like Exxon and Boeing. At the very least we can start being specific. Stop saying "special interests."

Let's face it: Americans are the most empowered people on the face of the Earth. All the transparency in the world isn't going to save us, though, if we are convinced that it is easier to destroy than to build. "Change" is yes-or-no referendum language. Not building language. That's fine. It was an election. Now we need to figure out how to build. Building is hard, but simple. It involves something we all know about—relationships. Here's a note from a friend out west:

"I think the Obama group initially tried to transform the campaign participation into local community action based on producing creative, localized solutions to real community problems, rather than waiting on Washington. But we don't get a sense that much has been done. Might be good to try to collect success stories and build on the places where this has worked. But it seems most of the Obama folks have become so tied up in Washington and Washington-sized problems that the real transformation in governance by increasing local-distributed responsibility has seemed to dry up, though I do believe that people should be more disappointed in themselves than in Obama. They didn't take up the challenge to be the change and have waited for him."

Sarah Palin made headlines for dissing law professors at the Tea Party convention. But she also said, "This is a beautiful movement because it is shaping the way politics are conducted... ." You know what? She's right. And we need to steal that line. We can start by figuring out how to connect with the people we're mad at right now. I guarantee you they have lots more in common with a typical progressive than the corporations who are fueling their cinematic irritation.

So take a Tea Partier to lunch. Don't laugh. These folks are angry for a reason (no jobs?). Many of them also believe in public purpose (what is self-governance but self-reliance?) and see it being ignored. Even rugged individuals live in communities. I grew up in a town of religious conservatives and they always helped me out. They changed my tires, cooked for me, took me to horse shows. They did this as my neighbor, despite being convinced that I and my California-born single-parented sisters and I were going straight to Hell. Progressives need to create a situation where we suspend our opinions and judgments in order to be able to listen to each other. Any community organizer can help out with this. Organize a couple of community dialogue events. Invite your member of Congress. Not to speak, to participate. Invite their local staff. Get good at it. Then invite people from the White House. We can make this contagious.

Most of us are tired of hearing each other's opinions. Could we actually have some real dialogue? In 2008, Obama advisor Marshall Ganz spoke of anchoring national goals locally through a new organization that could link action toward policy goals, facilitate local community collaboration, and offer the training, coordination, and communication that the campaign did so well.

How hard would it be to create this nonpartisan national network now? If there is one thing Americans are good at, it's talking to each other with a purpose. In fact, this could be your first topic at lunch.

GRAVEL PAVES THE ROAD TO THE WHITE HOUSE
by Megan Jordan, Velveteen Mind blog

The sound of gravel crunching under slow-moving tires is the sound of the small town to me. The sound of cicadas on a warm summer evening while you wave at your neighbors honking as they drive past your home. That is small-town life.

I grew up in a small town of 5,000 in southern Illinois. Our town was the metropolis of our county, or so it seemed to me. We were surrounded by towns whose populations made them more like villages, whose residents came to our town to shop at the Wal-Mart or go out to eat at the fancy new smorgasbord.

Separating those towns from ours were two-lane roads bordered by cornfields, soybean fields, cows, and hay bales. The only traffic lights were the blinking kind. You often had to pass tractors on the road or hold your tongue as you followed behind the Amish in their wagons. It was that kind of small town.

The phrase "small-town values" is being thrown around a lot lately. On one side of the aisle, you hear the declaration "We believe in small-town values." On the other side, you hear the question "But what *are* small-town values?"

Defining "small-town values" is as easy as defining what "love" is to a toddler. You know it when you feel it, but it is difficult to put into words, particularly when you find yourself on the spot facing a raised eyebrow and a smug smirk awaiting your sure-to-be fumbling explanation.

The question of small-town values and whether or not they are relevant or important is intriguing, regardless of your political leanings. The majority of our country, if not our world, is small towns. Much of the populations of our cities migrated from small towns. Small-town America is the root of this country, so what does that mean to us?

There is no one definition of what "small-town values" are, but to me it means a greater ability to see the people around you. Really *see* them.

Have you ever spent so much time online, for weeks at a time, that you find your head utterly filled with noise? You didn't notice it happening, but then you step outside one evening, discover it quiet, and realize that you had cocooned yourself within a wall of static?

Picture yourself working on your computer, appliances running in the kitchen, laundry running in the next room, kids watching TV, husband listening to his iPod ...and suddenly the power goes out. After much rummaging around for flashlights and grumbling about how you have so much to get done, you finally submit to the fact that you'll probably be in the dark for at least a few more hours, which no amount of huffing and puffing will change.

And then it happens. You realize that you've just had an eye-to-eye conversation with your kids that lasted longer than the time it takes to say, "In a minute..." or "As soon as I finish..." or "Tell me about that while I'm..."

Notice how they cut their eyes the way your grandmother used to when they say, "*I* have a good idea..." and then that idea is revealed to revolve around candy. The way they touch their hair when they are thinking of what to say next or tap their fingers together while anticipating your answer on that candy question still on the table.

It's easy to miss those details when you aren't even looking at them.

There is nothing to distract you from them and you find yourself able to *see* them. See them clearly. Hear them without the background hum of your modern life keeping you consistently 20-percent distracted.

That feeling is what small-town life is to me. It is a simplification, to be sure, but when compared to life in a large city, I think it is accurate. For me, at least.

Now take it a step further and imagine turning off the TV news and radio talk programs and Internet for two weeks. No newspapers, no magazines, nothing other than your personal world filling your attention. You still listen to music and watch movies, go out to dinner and take your kids to the park. But you aren't necessarily aware of what is going on a world away. You don't know about every tropical depression forming in the ocean and cease fire being negotiated over some sandy terrain.

I have done that. I can tell you first-hand how amazing it is to watch your priorities crystallize. To feel the stress drain away that you never knew was there, held in the base of your neck, stemming from problems that may or may not ever have anything to do with you.

You find yourself living your life, not a million other people's.

That firmly planted grounding of self and family and immediate community is small-town values to me.

I am not advocating ignorance. I'm not even advocating small-town life. Rather, I am trying to put my finger on what small-town values are by submerging myself in the feeling of a small town and reaching down to the core of *me*, asking "What do you see? How do you feel?"

I feel compassion on a personal level. I see community at its root. I am digging my hands into a foundation that is rich and firm, but that must be maintained in order to remain strong and fertile.

Without that strong foundation, we cannot build our tall towers that allow us to see those who were previously beyond our horizon and beyond our reach. Beyond our help.

Ask yourself, "What are small-town values?" Tell me why they are important. Tell me how we can ever help globally if we cannot first live a fully realized life locally.

Gravel paves the road to The White House. I struggle to articulate why that is important to remember, but my gut tells me that it is.

JOHN KENNEDY, BARACK OBAMA, TWO INAUGURATIONS AND TWO GENERATIONS OF DREAMERS
by Cynthia Samuels, Don't Gel Too Soon blog

I seem to be living in the WayBack Machine. Lots of memories of 1968 and even 1963. Now as January 20, 2009 approaches, yet another looms. January 20, certainly, but in 1961.

There was an almost-fifteen-year-old girl and her mother fresh off an overnight train from Pittsburgh, having arrived at Union Station in time to watch the Army flame-throwers melt a blizzard's worth of snow on the streets of the Washington, D.C. inaugural route, they make their way to their parade seats: in the bleachers, way down near the Treasury Building.

I spent most of 1960 besotted with John Kennedy. And Jackie. And Caroline. And all the other Kennedys who came with them. Most of my lunch money went to bus fare as, after school, I shuttled-back and forth "to town" to volunteer in the local JFK headquarters. I even had a scrapbook of clippings about Kennedy and his family. So. My parents surprised me with two inaugural parade tickets. My mom and I took the overnight train and arrived around dawn Inauguration morning. We couldn't get into the swearing-in itself, of course, so we went to a bar that served breakfast (at least that's how I remember it) and watched the speech on their TV. Then we made our way along the snowy sidewalks to our seats, arriving in time to watch the new president and his wife roll by, to see his honor guard, the last time it would be comprised solely of white men (since Kennedy ordered their integration soon after,) in time to see the floats and the Cabinet members and the bands and the batons.

It was very cold. We had no thermos, no blankets, nothing extra, and my mom, God bless her, never insisted that we go in for a break, never complained or made me feel anything but thrilled. Which I was. As the parade drew to a close and the light faded, we stumbled down the bleachers, half-frozen, and walked the few blocks to the White House fence. I stood there, as close to the fence as I am now to my keyboard, and watched our new president enter the White House for the first time as commander in chief.

That was half a century ago. I can't say it feels like yesterday, but it remains a formidable and cherished memory. It was also a defining lesson on how to be a parent; it took enormous love and respect to decide to do this for me. I was such a kid—they could have treated my devotion like a rock star crush, so young, they could have decided I would "appreciate it more" next time. (Of course there was no next time.) Instead, they gave me what really was the lifetime gift of being a part of history. And showed me that my political commitment had value—enough value to merit such an adventure.

Who's to say if I would have ended up an activist (I did)—and then a journalist (I did)—without those memories. If I would have continued to act within the system rather than try to destroy it (I did). If I would have been the mom who took kids to Europe, brought them along on news assignments to inaugurations and royal weddings and green room visits with the Mets (Yup, I did). I have learned to honor the interests and dreams of my children the way my parents had honored my own. So it's hard for me to tell parents now to stay home.

One good friend advised that "those with little children" skip Barack Obama's inaugural parade, since strollers and backpacks are banned for security reasons. I'm sure she's right. But if you've got a dreamer in your house, a young adult who has become a true citizen because of this election, I'd try to come. After all, he's *their* guy. What he does will touch their lives far more than it will ours. Being part of this beginning may determine their willingness to accept the tough sacrifices he asks of them and probably will also help to build their roles as citizens—as Americans—for the rest of their lives. And it will also tell them that, despite curfews and learner's permits, parental limit-setting and screaming battles, their parents see them as thinking, wise and effective people who will, as our new president promised them, help to change the world.

I'M BREAKING A PROMISE TO MYSELF
by Jodi, Jodifur blog

I had promised myself not to use my blog to talk about politics. Anyone who reads me knows what side I am on, and you don't read me to hear me spout off on my beliefs. I'm not judging others that use their blogs as a political spaces, but that's not really me. But something happened in 2008 that made me change my mind.

I work in a building that houses most of the social welfare programs for my county. The Women, Infants and Children Program, food stamps, energy assistance, you get my drift. And I need to point out—I work for an incredibly rich county. I pulled into my building at 9:15 a.m. and the parking lot was full. The satellite lot next door was also full and I parked on the street. That had become a usual occurrence in the fall of 2008, and has continued, even until this day.

When the elevator doors opened to the second floor, where the programs are located, the waiting room was packed and the line snaked around the room. These are people, in a rich county, who need help to pay for food, help to pay their electrical bills, help to secure the down payment for an apartment—or else be homeless.

Help.

When the Republicans were in office they cut these programs so much that there was not much money once a Democrat was elected. And with the economy, more people need help. Anyone who did not think the economy was in trouble during the time of the 2008 presidential election was sorely mistaken (John McCain, Sarah Palin, George W. Bush). I wish you could have seen the Department of Social Services in September 2008. Hey, I wish you could see the Department of Social Services now. Economic crises do not end the minute a new administration comes in. Too much damage has already been done.

I understand not everyone believes in social welfare; not everyone believes we should pay taxes to help people. That it is more important to fight unnecessary wars than it is to make sure people do not have to choose between gas for their cars or feeding their family. I am not that someone. I remember talking to a Republican (yes, I know some) before the last election and they told me the economy was not in crisis and that this was all made up by "the liberal media." That the "liberal media" was turning everything Sarah Palin said around to make her look unqualified. Um, Sarah Palin was unqualified. If she was qualified to be vice president then I am qualified to be attorney general. Hey, she was PTA president and I work in the County Attorney's office. She'll still be unqualified to be president in 2012, but I suspect she will run.

Fox News and the Republicans have done a very good job convincing people that every other media outlet other than Fox is biased. That when someone has the audacity to speak the truth that they are out to get him or her. It's a calculated effort, and I'm terrified that it's working and will continue to work in 2012.

What does "liberal media" mean anyway? Since when do we need to classify our media? Did the "liberal media" make up the stock market crash? The real estate bubble bursting? Was H1N1 really a ploy so Barack Obama could get his universal health-care plan passed? Do people really honestly believe these things?

A McCain administration went against everything I believe in. As an American, but also as a human being. We should not be invading countries when people in our own country are starving. When people cannot afford health care. When people cannot afford their electrical bills.

A McCain/Palin ticket terrified me on so many levels in 2008, and I'm even more scared to see what happens in 2012. I believe firmly in a woman's right to choose. Interestingly, McCain said in an interview, two days before he picked Palin, that he believed the Republican platform should be amended to allow abortion in cases of rape and incest and when a mother's life is at risk. That never happened, and he picked Palin who does not believe that. Hypocritical much? Pander to your base much?

I'd like to see a Republican candidate in 2012 who believes the things I believe in. That is the only way I would consider voting for anyone other than President Obama.

I want to pull into work in the morning and have my pick of spaces.

A BREAK UP LETTER
by Loralee Choate, Loralee's Looney Tunes blog

Dear GOP,

We've been together a really long time, haven't we? It was a beautiful relationship for sure.

Hey, remember the time that Bill Clinton was running for president and I loathed him and couldn't believe my fellow teenagers were falling for his saxophone playing on late night television? How mad I was that I would be eighteen on November 7th, which was FOUR FLIPPING DAYS after the elections and I was so pissed off they wouldn't let me vote for Bush that I practically picketed the registration office?

Man…those were the days, weren't they?

I've been raised with you. I remember watching the Reagan/ Carter debates and I knew who my man was even though I was only, what? Six?

My parents totally approved of you. Well, except for that weird period where they cheated on the elephant and ran around with the donkey during part of the Clinton administration. It was weird.

My mother's insistence that *"THAT WOMAN* chased and stalked our President!"* (when, hi...she was 21 and hello, due to that little thing called The Secret Service, nobody stalks the president of the United States unless HE WANTS TO BE STALKED) really, really confused me. Needless to say, I was highly relieved when they came to their senses and voted for Dubya in 2000.

Lately, though, you and I just haven't been getting along. The fights, the bickering, the distance.

I really think we've grown into two different people. And I have come to a decision:

I AM LEAVING YOU AND OFFICIALLY REGISTERING AS A DEMOCRAT.

I've been thinking really hard about us for a long time. I have gotten more and more vocal about ideas and thoughts and stands that I have stayed quiet about for a long time.

In the hundreds of times I have told my story about being invited to visit The White House to talk with Valerie Jarrett about our personal health care story, I keep uttering the phrase "I'm a moderate Republican."And I kept feeling more and more and more...wrong.

It used to be very true. I just don't think it is any longer.

Between the passing of Proposition 8 in California banning gay marriage (which I more strongly disagree with than I can find adequate words for) and health care, I have really had the foundations of my political ideals shaken.

In talking about my outrage with both of these issues (and others) I came to realize how important this is to me and how different my thinking is from many of the people around me. I am an extremely non-confrontational person but I have felt passionately enough about things lately to go to the mat with my nearest and dearest loved ones. I've gotten into heated, intense arguments with people I have never seriously argued with.

I find myself shaking my head more at the right and nodding it more at the left.

It used to be the exact opposite.

During a conference call through *BlogHer* with a Republican congresswoman, though she was lovely, I found myself yelling at the phone in frustration. When I hung up the phone it was like the last little piece of the puzzle was in place and I just absolutely, 100 percent KNEW.

I am worried, I will confess. I'm registering as a Democrat AND I'VE NEVER EVEN VOTED FOR ONE.

This is a HUGE change for me. It's almost like leaving a religion. But I know it's the right choice for me right now. When I end something it's usually pretty final. I may be able to work it out, but chances are high I will never feel the same about it again. So, I don't think my feelings about you will ever go back to what they once were.

Lots of things in my life are changing. I've outgrown things and I've seen others without the rose colored glasses I am prone to wearing. I owe it to myself to do this to see if I feel more comfortable. And frankly, I am doing your party NO favors by staying in it feeling the way that I do.

I don't even know if the Democrats would even WANT someone like me. I am pro-life (though that is a gray area and much too long for this post), I am ADAMANT about military funding, and I am really not sure if I love the Earth enough for the left side of the aisle. This decision IS NOT ISSUE BASED. It's because of the way I THINK.

After hundreds of hours of bickering, debating and arguing about the ins and outs of both parties I came to realize something: I have a completely different ideology then the party I have been a part of since I was eighteen. And it's too different to remain a Republican any longer.

So, I'm not.

Before we say goodbye I want to assure you I don't find either side "BAD." I love WAY too many people to bits and pieces that I believe are true, humble, lovely, classy and good-hearted to ever classify a whole party that way. You will find assholes on both sides, frankly.

So, thanks for all the memories, GOP. It was fun while it lasted.

If you're feeling all wounded and hurty over this, you can go cuddle with my husband. He's still there for you. AND...he's an excellent big spoon.

Kisses n' stuff,
Loralee

HAS DOOCE BECOME THE MODERN-DAY JUNE CLEAVER?
by Susan Getgood, Snapshot Chronicles blog

Before I begin, full disclaimer. These are my thoughts, my feelings, my perceptions about gender stereotypes. Your mileage may vary.

I'm 46. As your mileage catches up to mine, you may see my point of view. Or not.

Of late, the mainstream media has shifted its attention to the mom blogger. Whether it covers the "Digital Mom" (the *Today Show*) or the" "Secret Lives of Moms" (*Oprah*), it seems to be focusing its "laser" attention on a new stereotype of moms. A digital mom. One who seems to be in her early thirties, generally white and blond-ish, and blogging about her experiences—good, sometimes bad, and occasionally whiny—as a mom. She is generally played on TV by Heather Armstrong aka Dooce, perhaps the most famous "mom blogger."

Don't get me wrong. I love being a mom. I waited a long time to become one, and it was never certain that I would. My son is one of the most important things in my life.

But my experience of motherhood as a later-in-life mom with, at the time my son Douglas was born, a senior executive job at a technology company is very different than Heather's. I had to battle different things, including very real sexism on the job. I had to operate in a world where my joy in parenthood had to be tempered, because my male colleagues saw it as a weakness. They would never admit it, but oh my, was it clear. Seen, not heard, baby.

I have tremendous respect for women who, like Dooce, have turned their motherhood into a money stream. God bless you and rock on as you rake it in. Not for me, but it works for you and I have no problem with it.

I'm also NOT proposing that mom bloggers stop sharing their stories in any way they wish on their blogs. Your life, your stories, your words, your right. BUT…

Have we taken four steps forward and five steps back? Are we still letting mainstream media define us by our motherhood? Sure, it is not June Cleaver anymore; there's a nod to diversity. A teeny weeny nod.

Nevertheless, the media seems to be refocusing on women in a very traditional role of mother, tripping lightly over our other achievements. Have we really come a long way, or are we back near the beginning?

Is this new perception of modern-day moms damaging our ability to be perceived as women APART from our roles as mothers? The media seems to be grabbing hold of an image of the digital mom that threatens to overwhelm our individual and collective achievements as professional women. To stuff us back in a gender-defined box.

How else to explain shows like *In the Motherhood*? Or *Oprah's* "Secret Lives of Moms" episode, which I did not watch because the show generally irritates me and I didn't expect the mom episode to be much different. Is the digital mom becoming a new stereotype that will be just as damaging as June Cleaver?

I'm worried that the answer is 'yes.'

Now, here's where I put on my truly radical feminist hat. Be warned, and bear with me, as I am still thinking through this issue. I would love to hear your thoughts, whether you agree with me, think I am full of shit, or something in between.

Is the mainstream media stuffing women, in general, back in the mommy box because the U.S. power structure relies on women staying in their traditional gender role? To some degree, I think the answer is 'yes.'

Those in power—mostly men—want to stay in power. Full stop. Individual women are allowed to break out of the mold—if they push push push hard enough, give up everything except their careers etc. They are allowed to be the rare exceptions—the Queen Bees. They are unique.

Society doesn't acknowledge that women can be just as capable and competitive as their male counterparts, and still be nurturers.

Moms. The successful woman is special. [Note: Women are also allowed to rise to the top if they embody the stereotype and use it to be successful. Mary Kay, Avon, etc.]

The rest of us? At the core, The Powers That Be want—need—us as a gender to stay in the traditional role as much as possible. Our economy is to some degree built on the assumption that we will. We can have jobs, but not the top jobs. Look at the tech industry, even the social media industry. At most conferences, most of the speaking slots are STILL filled by men. A smattering of token women, usually the same ones over and over. Because, you know, they are special.

Even Michelle Obama, a very successful attorney in her own right, has been completely redefined as a wife and mother. Don't even get me started on how the media has f-ed over Hillary Clinton. That would take multiple posts and only my policy wonk friends would stick it out.

The other side of this problem is the Madonna -Whore dichotomy. It often seems, women must be one or the other. Never both. Our society still has tremendous difficulty separating sex from biology. Consider breastfeeding. Biology, people. Mothers make milk, and some choose to breastfeed their babies. Others don't. Has NOTHING to do with sex. No need for blankets. Or embarrassment. For anyone.

Yes, this mom-in-the-media trend makes me very uneasy. Tell me I'm wrong. I want to be wrong. I don't think I am.

BLOOD & POLITICS
by Lucia Davies, The New 30 blog

It has come to my attention, not for the first time, that someone in my family has been working hard to "save" me from myself and from my party of choice. This is her stance: she truly *believes* she knows what's best. She even sent me a book a couple of years ago entitled, *Useful Idiots: How Liberals Got it Wrong in the Cold War and Still Blame America First.*

At first, furious, I wanted to send it back to Amazon and have them credit her account. But upon reflection, I chose to do the opposite of taking the bait (something I could never have done when I lived with her). I simply never mentioned the book. Never mentioned receiving it. Never mentioned having tossed it into the garbage an hour after said receipt. This has not stopped her, however, in her quest. She frequently sends emails that are driven by such "excitable" celeblicans as Ann Coulter and Rush Limbaugh. She holds George W. Bush up to the sunlight and rather than see his flimsy, frat-boy, bullying character, she takes the gaps where the light shines through as heavenly auras. She's truly, madly deeply in love with Dick (The Dick) Cheney.

Only two days ago, we had a conversation about offshore drilling (she introduced the topic) wherein I was lectured about how the liberals, the Sierra Club nuts and Congress are behind the whole energy crisis. Mind you, our dependence on oil was in no way to blame. When I pointed out to her that the good news is there are clean energy alternatives, such as the fuel-cell car that Honda currently has on the road, it was as if I were handing her a bazooka to blow such good ideas away. "Then, it's going to rain ALL THE TIME. All that water vapor in the air? We'll never, NEVER have sunshine!" She then launched a diatribe citing all the other reasons why we need to drill in the Arctic and damn the polar bears (They've gone up there and looked around—*there aren't any animals up there!*").

Finally, I gently urged her to lay this conversation aside. That we would have to agree to disagree. Shocked silence. "Oh, you... disagree? Oh, well, Oh. Hmm. Well. I thought you agreed with me on this."

Gently, I responded in the negative. And we agreed to retire the subject. Which is leaps and bounds from the sandbox we used to play in. Oh, there was tension, alright. If we'd been using landline phones it would have crackled from the pop and hiss of simmering fury, on both sides. But the decision to leave it alone was a milestone—for myself and for her.

This morning, in my Weight Watchers meeting, the subject was "boundaries." The leader theorized that every crossing of boundaries is done to satisfy a need. The discussion got pretty personal. At one point, she said "Anybody else have boundary issues? Someone crossing your boundaries and making you crazy?" I never participate in these meetings, but today my hand shot up.

"It's been 45 years or so, and my mother is still trying to turn me into a Republican." The entire room erupted in gales of laughter. But the leader hushed everyone up.

"What need is she trying to meet?" she asked. I had never thought about it from that viewpoint. At first I said that she needed to have control of the situation, of me. But then, upon further investigation, we agreed that her need is that I be more like her. If my politics were a mirror of hers, that would bring us closer. When I looked at it that way, a new understanding, and even compassion, washed over me.

The cold hard facts? My mother is a rabid Republican and I am a yellow-dog Democrat, and we've never agreed on politics. We never will. But this new insight shows her attempts to sway my opinions can be attributed to a deep yearning for connection. Which, when I thought back on it, was clearly expressed at the end of our phone call.

"The first four years of your life, when it was just you and Dad and me," said my mother, "I find myself thinking about those years a lot these days. I loved you so much." The wistfulness in her voice knocked the wind out of me for a moment.

Bone-deep honesty from the person, as a child, I had loved more than anyone. The person I had learned, over the arc of our time together, to distrust. As had she. And finally, the person I have relearned how to trust. There are no politics when it comes to blood. It masquerades as politics. But it's not. Love isn't right or left or even down the middle. It's simply love, as complicated and intense as all get-out. It's not to be questioned or influenced or counted or praised, even. It simply is.

"I loved you so much, too, Mom." Before we hung up, we cried a little together. Something I don't think we've ever done before.

While I will vote the Democratic ticket in November, this may be the first election I won't think of my vote in terms of "canceling out" my mother's. And maybe, just maybe, she won't think of *her* vote that way, either.

PLEASE DON'T VOTE
by Sarah Braesch, Sarah and the Goon Squad blog

I know everybody is saying that you should go vote tomorrow but I don't want you to.

Here are three reasons.

1) If you don't vote, my vote counts more.
2) If you don't vote, I won't have to stand in line all day long. This is especially important if you live in my neighborhood.
3) I am scared that you might be voting for John McCain. While I personally don't have anything against John McCain and I think he would even make a pretty good president, he is old and Sarah Palin scares the crap out of me. If she were to end up appointing people to the bench, it could set back civil rights and women's rights for fifty years.

OK. The truth is I think you *should* vote.

The truth is that I am not a Democrat. I am an Independent.

The truth is that neither party represents my interests, but the Democrats come a lot closer.

The truth is that for the first time since 1992 I am voting *for* a presidential candidate instead of against one. For the first time since I have been old enough to vote I think that no matter who wins we are better off.

The truth is that no matter which ticket wins, history will be made.

The truth is that even though I think we have acted in an embarrassing fashion for the past seven years, I am still proud to be an American.

The truth is that I am excited for the election.

The truth is that I can't wait for it to be over so we can talk about something else.

The truth is that just by having the option to vote we all win.

But I still wasn't kidding about not voting if you live in my neighborhood. I'll be in line with two four-year-olds.

THE SOUTHERN GIRL'S GUIDE TO PROPER POLITICAL DISCOURSE: WHAT YOUR MOMMA SHOULD'VE TOLD YOU
by Shannon Lowe, Rocks in My Dryer blog

So, I don't know if you've heard, but they're thinking of electing a new president.

Of course you've heard. You couldn't have missed it, with all the shouting from both sides (we are a nation of equal-opportunity meanies). Some of the vitriol I've seen and read has made me feel suddenly less alarmed by the scuffles that sometimes erupt in the back of my mini-van.

I know you've heard of political correctness, the idea of conducting yourself in a way to "minimize offense". You might think that notion was invented by the media, or sociologists. But you would be wrong.

It was invented by Southern women.

We've made "minimizing offensiveness" an art form. We do it all day. We are trained to do it at our mothers' knees. In fact, I remember, quite distinctly, my parents telling me never, *ever* to bring up politics or money in conversation unless you were absolutely certain where the other person stood. And even then, you should proceed carefully.

Since I have received such fine training myself, I thought I would offer up the following to the Whole Entire Internet, or At Least The Portion That Blogs About Politics.

1. Do not make assumptions that the person you're talking with must vote a certain way because of her gender, race, religion, or shoe size. That simply tells your conversation partner that you don't think she's smart enough to make up her own mind, and that is just plain tacky. Anyway, you know what they say about assumptions....well, I'll let you look that one up on your own.

2. To expand on #1, when you begin a political discussion with a stranger or acquaintance, do not launch into a tirade about how horrible Senator Joe Don is, because this stranger might be *voting* for Joe Don. Heck, your stranger might have a Daddy whose old football coach once had his hair cut by Joe Don's niece. It *is*

the South, you know.

3. Name-calling is completely, always inappropriate. But if you really feel you *must* throw around words such as "socialist" and "radical right-wing nut-job," it would soften things a bit if you would insert a "bless his heart" at the end of sentence.

4. When you go to the polls in November, please do not wear white shoes, because it is after Labor Day. It has nothing to do with politics, but I just needed to squeeze it in.

5. Do not use blanket statements of fact: "ALL Republicans are money-hungry," or "ALL Democrats are overly emotional," or "ALL Texans have big hair." Blanket statements are almost never true, and they just make the speaker sound desperate and uninformed. And anyway, I've known plenty of Texans whose hair size was only slightly above average.

6. It's OK to disagree with someone and still like them. Even if they're voting for the Other Guy, or—worse—cheering for the University of Texas football team. (I know. I'm bagging on Texas a little. They're big, they can handle it.)

7. Be charming. If you find yourself utterly and completely annoyed, then make a joke. If charming doesn't work, head straight for that great old friend of Southern women, *passive-aggressiveness*. You could even, perhaps, and I'm speaking purely hypothetically here, write a blog post about it.

BIRTH OF A LIBERAL
by Glennia Campbell, The Silent I blog

I've been thinking about how invested and involved I am in this election, probably more so than any election since my first time as a voter and of how it all started for me. That was way back in 1980, when I was a sophomore at Barnard College in New York. Since it was my first time, I looked at the candidates carefully. I didn't consider myself a Democrat or a Republican. I was the product of a mixed marriage (Dad's a Republican, Mom's a Democrat). I liked Jimmy Carter as a person, but as a president, he fell short of expectation. With the Iranian hostage crisis, gas rationing, and all the economic problems of the late '70's, it seemed like someone else could do a better job.

The problem was, the alternative was even scarier. I remember watching a video of Ronald Reagan driving through the California countryside, pointing out the window and saying, "I expect that someday this could all be ashes...all be gone...if the Soviets get their way. We have to build up our nuclear arsenal to make sure that doesn't happen."

He was so calm, so matter-of-fact. He scared the crap out of me. He was basically saying, "We'd better get them, before they get us." The idea that this guy would be in charge of nuclear weapons, or even a water pistol, gave me nightmares.

The minister at my church remarked after one of the Reagan-Carter debates that it was like watching "the evil of two lessers." I could not have agreed with him more. I wanted so much to really believe in a candidate, to volunteer to help out, but I just couldn't bring myself to do it.

Another candidate appeared on the scene. He made sense to me. He was a former Republican congressman, a social liberal and fiscal conservative who became an independent candidate for president. His name was John Anderson.

I had pretty much decided that he was my guy, when one of my college classmates pointed out to me that he was taking votes away from Carter, which would lead to a Reagan victory. He noted that if Reagan got into office, I could kiss my government-subsidized student loans, my work-study job, and my Pell grants goodbye. Reagan was promising to cut all these "unnecessary social programs" in favor of building up the nuclear arsenal to kill Russians, according to my classmate.

Without those loans and grants, there was no way my blue-collar family could afford to send me to college. I had visions of returning to my small Ohio hometown and working at the check-out stand at Kroger's during the day and going to community college at night. I had nearly killed myself in high school to get into Barnard, so this was not exactly what I had in mind for my future.

Still, I was going to vote with principle, and held steadfast to my commitment to John Anderson.

Voting day finally arrived, and I was excited to be voting for the very first time, a voting virgin. I stepped boldly into the voting booth and pulled the lever that shut the curtain behind me. I stared at the ballot for a long time. I started to sweat. The face of my classmate swirled in my head like a ghostly apparition... *"You can kiss those student loans goodbye..." "No more Pell grants..."*

I'm sure that the elderly League of Women Voters volunteers outside the booth were probably wondering what the hell I was doing in there all that time. I thought I was going to be sick.

Finally, I made my decision. Principle gave way to self-interest. I voted for Carter.

In the end, my emotionally traumatic voting experience didn't matter that much. Ronald Reagan won, and I spent the next eight years going to protest rallies against pretty much every foreign policy decision he made, from the escalation of the nuclear arms race to U.S. intervention in El Salvador to the covert war in Nicaragua. Standing up to Ronald Reagan made me a liberal and proud.

Twenty-eight years later, I'm still a liberal and still proud. I've voted in every election, every primary, and most local elections since then. Most of them are a blur, but as they say, "you never forget your first time."

SLEEPING WITH THE ENEMY
by Darryle Pollack, I never signed up for this...blog

Like my children, who were born to be Democrats, I was, too. I've written about my crush on John F. Kennedy, working for George McGovern, and taking Alli to meet Bill Clinton. My politics are no secret. But there is one thing I've kept secret and never mentioned all this time. Something kind of embarrassing. And with the election almost upon us, I guess I can't wait much longer to just come out with it and confess.

I've written a lot about my husband V—our marriage, anniversary, even his relationship with my ex-husband—and I've always portrayed him as a great guy. Which he is. But along with the great things about him, came this one little detail—like me, V is a product of his background, the flip side of mine—which means that I married a conservative Republican.

I never signed up for this, of course. I might have been more likely to marry an ax-murderer. Although I'm sure ax-murderers can have some very nice qualities. As I discovered Republicans can. At least this Republican.

The nice qualities were what allowed me to overlook the Republican issue when V and I got married. I had come out of a marriage to H, who was a Democrat; but towards the end of the marriage began voting Republican. I'm not saying it was the reason for our divorce, but it didn't help. And since I'd already technically been married to a covert Republican, it didn't seem like such a huge leap to marry another one. At least, not at the time.

And in the early days with V, this was not a big issue. When you're dealing with blended families and a life-threatening illness, party politics don't loom large over the marital bed.

Once it was clear that I was going to survive cancer, we settled into a Mary Matalin/James Carville kind of life, only less public. V's family and friends were mostly Republican and knew about my blue blood, but in their presence, I tried to keep my outrage to a low simmer. V's party affiliation was never a problem with my side. My family and friends are more opinionated and vocal—and V can barely get a word in, no matter what we are talking about. If he wore his Republican heart on his sleeve, V would just get his sleeve torn off.

So I was blue; he was red; we never became purple. Our votes cancelled each other out, and we tended to avoid intense political debates. My main strategy consisted of diversionary tactics: inventing errands for V on Election Day or distracting him so he would forget to go to the polls.

And politics was only one of our many differences. He's a WASP; I'm Jewish. He's a morning person; I'm a night owl. I blurt out whatever I'm thinking without thinking. V never blurts. He thinks. He's a "still-waters-run-deep" guy. And I don't usually know what's going on in those still waters.

Another difference is that V's very low key and I'm more a drama queen. So I might walk in the door and announce, "Guess what!! Something amazing happened today!! I won five dollars in the lottery!!" Whereas V is the kind of person who would look up in the middle of dinner and say calmly, "Oh, I forgot to tell you. I won the Nobel Prize two days ago."

So it was entirely in keeping with our characters that a few years ago, I opened the mail one day and saw one of those Democratic Party fund-raising mailers. The thing was, the name at the top wasn't mine. It was V's name. Which is how I learned that my Republican husband was now a registered Democrat.

It took me 10 years of marriage to lay the groundwork, George W. Bush and Dick Cheney managed to push him over the top, and V cast his first Democratic vote for John Kerry in 2004.

I have no complaints about V's lack of fanfare. We didn't even open a bottle of champagne to mark the occasion. But we have plenty to celebrate. Especially this year. V supported Barack Obama right from the beginning, andI get towatch this unbelievable election season unfolding, and share it with a kindred spirit.

We never really had any screaming matches during the ten years we were on opposite sides. But being completely honest, I think V made his conversion just in time. I'm not sure our marriage could have survived him voting for Sarah Palin.

GIVING OBAMA MY VOTE–BUT NOT MY CHEST
by Liz Gumbinner, MOMocrats blog

As I watched history being made on CNN during the 2008 campaign, I thought to myself , where is my Barack T-shirt? . Where's my *My Mama's for Obama* baby onesie? Where's my *Obama for Change* potholder? My *Barack & Roll* boxer shorts?

Where's my *Obama is My Homeboy* trucker cap?

It's not like me not to wear my heart–or my candidate–on my sleeve, as my junk drawer scattered with worn Wes Clark, Al Gore, and John Kerry memorabilia would indicate. Deep in my closet somewhere, I even have the Hillary Clinton silkscreen tee that I proudly purchased at Marc Jacobs in my perkier-boobed days during her

Senate run in New York. I think it's a size negative 12.

But last week I pulled the lever for Obama. So why no Hanes Beefy-T with his likeness on the chest? I had to think hard.

Looking back at my political memorabilia, my buttons were as much a vote for the candidates as a vote for "not the other guy." My support of John Kerry may have been lukewarm at best—though God help me, I would have killed to have Theresa up there as First Lady—but my support for Not Bush was fierce and strong and unwavering.

And suddenly it became clear to me.

I may have pulled for Obama, butI'm not prepared to say "Not Hillary." I burst into tears when I saw a woman's name up to the right of the squeaky old lever in the voting booth last Tuesday. I still have some conflicted feelings for not having supported her. (Yes, I'm sup-posed to be bigger and cooler and smarter than that, but I guess I'm not.) And if indeed she's the candidate, I'll campaign for her like nobody's business.

But until then, I'm perfectly content to join the 70 percent of Democrats who agree that we've got two fine choices this year. And until one of them is the nominee, I think I'll keep my wardrobe slogan-free.

THIS IS WHERE I DEFEND MICHELE BACHMANN
by Jessica Pieklo, Hegemommy blog

Michele Bachmann is at it again, it appears. And I'm not talking about her "unusual" alternate 2011 State of the Union rebuttal, nor am I talking about her nails-on-a-chalkboard partisan shriek during that rebuttal. I'm talking about the fact that her presence alone has the effect of keeping women maligned in mainstream politics.

Let's take a step back here. Bachmann is the leader of the con-gressional Tea Party Caucus and has apparently stepped into the vacuum left by the other darling of the hard right, Sarah Palin. But un-like Palin, who is principally a media presence, Bachmann is an actual elected representative. And the Tea Party is her natural constituency. She's ambitious and determined to make herself a national leader and has plenty of backers who believe she can do just that.

But despite her hard-right pedigree and her ambition, both the mainstream media and the Republican leadership dismiss Bachmann as a "bobblehead" who makes "unusual" decisions. She's often referred to as "crazy" and "dumb" by the left. But Michele Bachmann is not crazy. And she's not dumb.

Instead, she's everything we want an elected official to be—to a certain degree. She's loyal to her constituents and eager to climb the ranks in Washington. She shows a degree of media savvy that Speaker of the House John Boehner could sure use. But for whatever reason we, the collective political public, seem unable or unwilling to applaud her for these efforts and instead attack her personally.

Why? Because she's a woman.

I'll go ahead and duck while some of you throw tomatoes now.

Why not talk about the insanity of her positions as opposed to the insanity of her character? Let's talk about the factual misstatements she makes (and there are plenty) and demand she answer to them, rather than dismiss her as "stupid." Hell, let's start simple and just make sure *Politico* consistently spells her name correctly. Let's start with the basic assumption that the woman is smart enough to get elected and to stay there, which means, at a fundamental level, even Michele Bachmann demands some respect.

Make no mistake about it, I think the positions this woman holds are dangerous and the policies she endorses are draconian. But that doesn't mean I'm comfortable with just how quickly Bachmann is dismissed and how disposable she's been treated, both by Democrats and Republicans. Would Boehner have been so blasé with a "whatever" attitude if former Congressman Tom Tancredo delivered remarks in addition to Congressman Paul Ryan? Would MSNBC's Chris Matthews call him a "balloon head," despite the fact that Tancredo has made a pretty damn good living off of playing fast and loose with historical fact as Bachmann has done? I don't think so. And I'm not the only one.

THE YEAR OF THE WOMEN
by Donna Schwartz Mills, SoCal Mom blog

It is being said that our presidential election will be decided by women. We are 52 percent of the population and an even larger proportion of the population of actual voters. That's why both major political parties are going out of their way to sway undecided women.

But this post is NOT about politics. I prefer to voice those opinions over at the *MOMocrats* blog. I only mention it because it's part of a larger picture, where the media-at-large appears to have finally noticed that we women exist, as opinion-shapers and a powerful economic force in our own right.

And I hope you will excuse me while I bask in this.

You see, at 52 years old, I really feel like I have lived the modern women's revolution. I have fairly clear memories of 1963, the year Betty Friedan published *The Feminine Mystique*. I remember feeling inferior because my mom told me I was too dark-skinned to ever dye my hair blonde, which meant that I would never have fun, because that's what Clairol told me on TV. I wanted to be Miss America when I grew up, because she was the national ideal of grown-up womanhood.

Fortunately, my mom never told me that I would likely be too short and ethnic to ever be a candidate. And by the time I was 12, I realized that I was too cool anyway to pursue that particular dream. That was the year the nascent women's liberation movement protested the pageant by throwing "items of female torture" into a garbage can—and earned the colorful label of "bra burners."

To quote another advertisement from my childhood, we've come a long way, baby. OK, so the Equal Rights Amendment got shot down by Phyllis Schlafly and her posse of moral alarmists. But after Hillary Clinton's historic presidential candidacy and the media frenzy surrounding the Republicans' choice for vice president, women are being actively courted—and not just by advertisers.

Suddenly, our opinions matter.

I've seen more media requests for women in the last couple of weeks than I have in the entire five years I've been writing this blog: One of my *MOMocrat* sistahs was interviewed by CBS, and one was interviewed by Fox News and CNN.

They want our opinions. They want our support. They create products they hope will appeal to us. It's too bad they don't respect us.

Take the new movie, *The Women*. It is based on Claire Booth Luce's 1936 play (and 1939 MGM film) about society women, which was revolutionary at the time for its all-female cast.

Seventy years later, that all-female cast thing is still unique. In fact, it was one of the reasons writer/director Diane English (who created *Murphy Brown*) spent 14 years getting the thing made: no one wanted to green light a project that did not include one male character—because WHO would want to see it?

You see, there is a fallacy among the people who produce motion pictures that the only people who want to go out to movies any longer are men aged 25 and younger. A few months ago, most of the entertainment media was shocked at how successful the *Sex & the City* movie was. After all, it was a *chick flick*. And this summer, they were surprised again when *Mamma Mia* surpassed their box office projections.

Neither of these films got very good reviews. News flash: Movies created for women and families are not deemed "cool" by a lot of entertainment critics. A movie appealing to these audiences has to be Oscar quality to get an embrace. The rest are received with little praise, even the ones that fulfill their meager promise to be an entertaining diversion (and I think that's the goal of most films and for most filmgoers).

I am expecting that *The Women* won't be treated any better by the critics. I also expect that it will do very well at the box office. Because this is, after all, our year.

AN OPEN LETTER TO THE NEW YORK TIMES ABOUT MOM BLOGGERS, WOMEN WRITERS & THE UNIVERSE
by Joanne Bamberger, PunditMom blog

Dear *New York Times* (other mainstream media outlets, you should probably pay attention, too),

I'm so weary of your attempts to marginalize women writers online who happen to be mothers that I almost couldn't write this letter.

But I realized that if I didn't, I would feel guilty about not trying to change things so that if my fourth-grader ever wants to be a mother and a professional, maybe she won't have to fight this battle.

Was it really necessary to write a story on a professional blogging conference with the title "*Honey, Don't Bother Mommy. She's Busy Building Her Brand*?" The headline alone drips with mocking condescension that says to the world it's perfectly acceptable to continue belittling women for doing exactly the same things that men are doing in the online world today.

We've come a long way? Not.

"*Girly-bonding*?" I suspect that when the Google guys get together, no one on the *Times* staff would dare to suggest it was anything other than a serious business meeting. Hold an event where mothers do the same thing, and it's instantly a hen party. A "*modern day coffee-klatsch*?" Really? If I have coffee with the Kirtsy ladies or the MOMocrats it's a "*coffee-klatsch*," but espresso with Rick Sanchez about being one of the first bloggers on his now influential Twitter List would grab more of your attention?

I shouldn't be surprised. For decades, most of society has tried to push mothers who want to work, achieve, help support their families or speak out on issues to the side. In the 1950s and 1960s, it was acceptable for mothers to work for "pin money," but society was skeptical of how allowing women into certain jobs would impact men's control over the world. It's one thing to look back through today's *Mad Men* lens and chuckle about how amazing it was for the guys to allow Peggy Olson to become an actual copy writer! It's another, though, to suggest in 2010 that women who are trying to build careers and money-making opportunities, or using one of the few writing avenues available to them without any male barriers to entry, are somehow undeserving of respect for the simple reason that they've decided to procreate.

I realize your writer was probably trying to pen a humorous piece about a recent blog conference where women who are mothers (*GASP!*) gathered to hone their skills on search engine optimization, marketing, and earning a living through their blogs. Maybe you couldn't get past the name Bloggy Boot Camp to see what women were trying to accomplish.

But was it really necessary to add that gigantic cartoon graphic portraying this group of women are nothing more than carpool chaueffers and cooks tied to their PDA's and laptops to further make fun of us?

Are mothers we really still just about kids, toys, pets, and coffee?

If you had written a piece about the heavily male-attended South by Southwest Interactive conference with similar "daddy" art, I'm betting you'd have gotten a pretty seething letter from those organizers. Conferences like Netroots Nation are well-respected by the media. But when you write about gatherings like BlogHer, Bloggy Boot Camp, and others, we can feel the virtual pat on the head that says, "*There, there dear. Why don't you just write about your play dates and leave the important political writing to someone else!*"

To use faux humor and mockery to imply to millions of readers that mothers clearly shouldn't be out in the world trying to improve their families' economic lives or their careers is outrageous. To imply that we should be staying at home, tending to the kids and the man of the house, letting all those important conversations about building online businesses to the menfolk—you know, fathers like Guy Kawasaki and Markos Moulitsas—is insulting.

Of course, maybe it's just because you're afraid of what the future holds for the *New York Times* and that if you don't smack down the competition, your failing business model will run out of gas sooner than you'd like.

It's not just me. Other well-respected online women writers (I really prefer that term to "mommy bloggers") are annoyed with your attempts to, again, portray women online as moms having a hobby rather than the professionals we are. Even the positioning of stories about women online shows your inner disdain—we get the fashion and style section; SXSW and Guy Kawasaki get the technology or business sections.

I was also wondering: did your reporter bother to dig a little deeper with the women who attended Bloggy Boot Camp? Did she try to find out how many attendees were women with professional degrees and careers? It might shock you, but my online writing *is* my profession. I have more than a decade of experience in broadcast journalism, and I practiced law for 15 years. I make money with my "traditional" writing, I have written op-ed pieces for newspapers, and I am writing a book for which I have an enthusiastic publisher (no, don't assume it's a traditional "mom" topic—that will only get you into more hot water). I've even spoken at a variety of conferences you would deem worthy of respect.

Oh, yeah, I'm also a mother. And I'm not ashamed to incorporate my mother's perspective into my professional writing.

I know that somehow in the vaunted opinion of the *New York Times*, my motherhood makes me somehow less worthy, even though I have two hard-earned degrees. When I was a girl, I thought we would be past these motherhood stereotypes at this stage of the game. But being sad won't stop me from continuing to build my brand, my business, and my livelihood online, even though you will probably continue your antiquated and outdated ways of covering professional and political women.

My consolation is that every day there are more women writing online, creating businesses and building something tangible for their futures. And that puts us one step closer to world domination.

Don't worry, though. We're moms—we'll be benevolent dictators.

Sincerely yours,
Joanne Bamberger, aka PunditMom

CONCLUSION

When I started writing this book, I knew from talking with so many women over the last five years—that's when I first stuck my toes into the waters of the online world of social media—that mothers were the new political force to be reckoned with. The advent of social media tools and a relatively new online world with no barriers to entry changed in a moment how women and mothers could become activists, giving them the tools to embrace their political power more openly and collectively than they ever had before. The world of blogging became the new town center for mothers where they could write about anything and everything, finding power in that and using it to further their inner politicos in real life. But few in the mainstream media and political worlds were aware of that trend.

Then the Alaskan cyclone of Sarah Palin

and her version of political motherhood became one of *the* pop culture topics of 2010, leading many observers to assume that when mothers got political, they all became conservative "mama grizzlies." That phenomenon both helped and hindered mothers with less media visibility—it brought increased attention to political mothers as never before, but little focus to the motherhood experiences that awakened us to the possibilities of using our voices. As more women use their online spaces to promote the causes and politicians they believe in, the concept of political mothers will widen and, in time, we will stop being called "soccer moms" or "Wal-Mart moms," and, instead, be seen as political players with real influence.

As for women running for office, we're stuck—women still only make up about 17 percent of Congress. Studies show that regardless of the power we believe we have in other parts of our lives, women still hold back when it comes to seeking elective office because we don't see ourselves as qualified and we're afraid to fail. The good news is that programs to encourage and train women to run for office abound. Women of Generation Y and younger, like 29-year-old Krystal Ball, are seeing that running for office isn't as scary as it first seems and that even if we lose a race, we still win at moving the cause of women and mothers forward.

Mothers have a unique perspective that would benefit our male-heavy world of politics. I wouldn't go so far as some candidates in suggesting that motherhood is a necessary qualification for public office. But I would say that women whose worlds and world views have been changed by motherhood can offer insight and perspectives that our political world sorely needs. Putting our mom voices out there to advocate for issues that are important to us, and having that work published, read, and discussed will be the launching pad for a rejuvenated women's political involvement—on both sides of the aisle.

ACKNOWLEDGMENTS

I've long dreamed of writing a book. When I created the Mothers of Intention feature at my site PunditMom, I didn't know it would take me on a journey of discovering the true political side of mothers in a way that few were focused on or that it would turn into a book examining a growing phenomenon that is still little recognized by the mainstream. At first, I thought it would be a collection of essays, but then the book grew into an inspiring journey of examining how women with children were embracing their growing activist clout, yet were still getting such short political shrift or mainstream media attention. It's been an amazing experience to put this together and I hope that the research and the essays will shine a big spotlight on the fact that political mothers are here to stay.

There are a multitude of people in my life who encouraged and supported me through this process, and there's no way I can thank them all in a few short paragraphs. But I do have some who deserve my special thanks and gratitude.

First, this book would not have been possible without all the amazing contributors who believed in this project and who generously allowed me to include their essays here to show the world once and for all that mothers are the new political rock stars to be reckoned with in America, and that we were already that before the media fascination with the so-called "mama grizzlies."

Mothers of Intention wouldn't be the book that it turned into without the wise input and gentle guidance of my editor Lucy Chambers, as well as everyone at my publisher Bright Sky Press. Lucy encouraged me and gave me the confidence to create something bigger and bolder than I originally imagined, while all the other fabulous BSP people supported me and helped me through what sometimes felt like an unending publishing process!

I would not have met Lucy if my friend Laurie Smithwick hadn't introduced us at the very first Mom 2.0 Summit in 2009. Without Laurie convincing Lucy that she should talk with me, I'm not sure this book would have been in anyone's hands.

In addition to the essay contributors, many women shared their personal political journeys and experiences for my research, many of which is included in the book. I am grateful to them for taking the time out of their already busy schedules to share those stories, as well as to the friends who helped me track them down!

One of the biggest support networks I have in my life comes from my sisters in social media, even the ones who don't always agree with me politically. I have been inspired and supported by so many women I first met online by reading their blogs and websites, and later met in real life. There just isn't room here for me to thank every one of those fabulous women, but I am always grateful for their presence in my life and the encouragement I received from them all. I especially have to thank all my *MOMocrat* co-conspirators and my terrific friends in *The DC Moms* blogging community. But some women I do need to thank by name are Jill Miller Zimon, Cindy Samuels, Ilina Ewens, Caroline Jorgenson, Corina Fiore, Stephanie Himel-Nelson, Veronica Arreola, Susan Getgood, and Gloria Feldt. I am grateful to all of you for being real-life Mothers of

Intention who have inspired me in my political and literary journey.

Three people who have helped me think about the marketing and promotional aspects of being an author are my friends David Wescott, Carol Schiller, and Eric Kuhn—I can't thank them enough for the amazing hand-holding they so generously gave me to focus on the business side of being an author.

And I have to say a very special thank you to a writer I have long admired, Connie Schultz, who so kindly gave of her own limited time to write the preface for this book, a gift I will always treasure. I have been a fan of Connie's writing for a very long time and felt like a literary groupie when I was fortunate enough to meet her at a writing conference some years ago. Connie often generously reached out to encourage me in my writing efforts, keeping me focused on the overwhelming work of research and writing. And when I would start to hyperventilate, she reminded me that this was the journey I was meant to be on right now.

Finally, and most especially, I owe my biggest thanks to my husband David and our daughter, Rachel, for their endless patience, love, understanding, and support as I spent hours upon hours thinking, researching, writing, editing, and "birthing" *Mothers of Intention*. They knew that becoming an author was a dream I'd held in my heart for a long, long time. Without them, I could never have seen my dream come true. I just hope they will be as understanding if, and when, the idea for my next book strikes.

RESOURCES

Interested in getting in touch with your own inner "Mother of Intention?" Here's a list of a few resources to help you get started:

2012 Project, **www.cawp.rutgers.edu/education_training/2012Project/index.php**

Activism, Media & Politics Summit, **www.ampsummit.com**

American Association of University Women, **www.aauw.org**

American University, Women and Politics Institute, **www.american.edu/spa/wpi/ www.american.edu/spa/wpi**

BlogHer, **www.blogher.com**

Conservative Political Action Conference, **www.conservative.org/cpac**

Elect Women Magazine, **www.electwomen.com**

Emerge America, **www.emergeamerica.org**

EMILY's List, **www.emilyslist.org**

Feminist Majority Foundation, **www. http://feministmajority.org**

Independent Women's Forum, **www.iwf.org**

MOMocrats, **www.momocrats.typepad.com**

MomsRising, **www.momsrising.org**

National Coalition of Black Civic Participation, **www.hcbcp.org**

National Council of Negro Women, **www.ncbcp.org**

National Organization for Women, **www.now.org**

National Women's Political Caucus, **www.nwpc.org**

Netroots Nation Conference, **www.netrootsnation.org**

New Leader's Council, **www.newleaderscouncil.org**

Personal Democracy Forum, **www.personaldemocracy.com**

Rutgers Center for American Women and Politics, **www.cawp.rutgers.edu/index.php**

She Should Run Project, **www.sheshouldrun.org**

Smart Girl Summit, **www.smartgirlsummit.com**

Susan B. Anthony List, **www.sba-list.org**

The Barbara Lee Family Foundation, **www.barbaralee.com**

The George Washington University School of Political Management, **www.gspm.gwu.edu**

The Southeastern Institute for Women in Politics, **www.scelectswomen.com**

The White House Project, **www.thewhitehouseproject.org**

Voto Latino, **www.votolatino.org**

Women Who Tech, **www.womenwhotech.com**

Women's Campaign Forum, **www.wcfonline.org**

Women's Media Center, **www.womensmediacenter.com**

BLOG LIST

a moon, worn as if it had been a shell,
www.elizabethaquino.blogspot.com

About.com, www.womensissues.about.com

Amandatory Reading,
www. amandatoryreading.blogspot.com

Attack of the Redneck Mommy,
www.theredneckmommy.com

Care2, www.care2.com

Connie Schultz,
www.cleveland.com/schultz

Current Mom, www.currentmom.com

Diana Prichard, www.dianaprichard.com

Dirt and Noise, www.dirtandnoise.com

Don't Gel Too Soon,
www.dontgelyet.typepad.com

Down to Earth Mama, www.dtemama.com

Halushki, www.halushki.com

Hegemommy, www.hegemommy.com

I Never Signed Up for This ...,
www.blog.darrylepollack.com

Jessica Gottlieb, www.jessicagottlieb.com

Just a Conservative Girl,
www.912member.blogspot.com

Lawyer Mama, www.lawyermama.com

Huffington Post, Lorelei Kelly blog,
www.huffingtonpost.com/lorelei-kelly

Liza Was Here, www.lizawashere.com

Mamma Loves..., www.mammaloves.com

MaNNaHaTTaMaMMa,
www. mannahattamamma.com

Mojo Mom, www.mojomom.com

Mom-101, www.mom-101.com

MOMocrats, momocrats.typepad.com

MomsRising, www.momsrising.org

Morningside Mom,
www.morningsidemom.com

Motherhood Uncensored, www.
motherhooduncensored.typepad.com

Odd Time Signatures,
www.drumsnwhistles.com

Parentopia, www.parentopia.net/blog

PBS Parents/Supersisters,
www.pbs.org/parents/supersisters

PunditMom, www.punditmom.com

Rocks in My Dryer, www.rocksinmydryer.
typepad.com

Sarah and the Goon Squad,
www.sarahandthegoonsquad.com

Scrambled Cake,
www.scrambledcake.blogspot.com

Selfish Mom, www.selfishmom.com

Snapshot Chronicles,
www.snapshotchronicles.com

SoCal Mom, www.socalmom.net

The Dana Files, www.danafiles.com

The Girl Revolution,
www.thegirlrevolution.com

The Karianna Spectrum,
www.karianna.us/blog

The MomSlant, www.themomslant.com

The New 30, www.thenew30.typepad.com

The Silent I, www.thesilenti.com

The State of Discontent,
www.thestateofdiscontent.com

The Stir by Café Mom,
thestir.cafemom.com

This Woman's Work,
www.thiswomanswork.com

Uppercase Woman,
www.uppercasewoman.com

Velveteen Mind, www.velveteenmind.com

Viva La Feminista,
www.vivalafeminista.com

Writes Like She Talks,
www.writeslikeshetalks.com

*Xiaolin Mama,*www.xiaolinmama.com

1   Shelley J. Correll, Stephen Benard, In
    Paik,"Getting a Job: Is There a Motherhood
    Penalty?," *American Journal of Sociology* 112,
    no. 5 (March 2007): 1297–1338; Shelley J.
    Correll, interview on February 2, 2010; Ruth
    Schechter, "Motherhood Penalty Remains
    a Pervasive Problem in the Workplace,
    "November 22, 2009, http://www.stanford.edu/
    group/gender/cgi-bin/wordpressblog/2009/11/
    motherhood-penalty-remains-a-pervasive-
    problem-in-the-workplace/.

2   Based on participation in live interview
    with pollsters on this CNN segment, http://
    johnkingusa.blogs.cnn.com/2010/09/29/to-
    night-on-jkusa-walmart-moms/?iref=allsearch;
    Grace J. Yoo, Emily H. Zimmerman, and
    Katherine Preston, "The Obama Effect:
    Multidisciplinary Renderings of the 2008
    Campaign," in *Mothers Out to Change U.S.
    Politics: Obama Mamas Involved and Engaged,*
    ed. Heather Harris, Kimberly Moffitt,
    Catherine Squires, (State University of New
    York Press, 2010); Jill S. Greenlee, "Soccer
    Moms, Hockey Moms, and the Question of
    Transformative Motherhood," *Politics and
    Gender (2010).*

3   Motrin Moms Commercial, http://www.you-
    tube.com/watch?v=BmykFKjNpdY.

4   Swiffer Commercial, http://www.youtube.com/
    watch?v=9_JpYfScoHs.

5   Donna St. George, "Most Stay-at-Home
    Moms Start That Way," *Washington Post,*
    October 1, 2009, http://www.washingtonpost.
    com/wp-dyn/content/article/2009/09/30/
    AR2009093005106.html?hpid=topnews; Cathy
    Arnst, "The Opting Out Myth," *Bloomberg
    Business Week Online,* June 24, 2008, http://
    www.businessweek.com/careers/workingpar-
    ents/blog/archives/2008/06/the_opting-out.
    html.

6   Leslie Bennetts, "The Meaning of Meryl,"
    Vanity Fair, January 2010.

7   *The Byline Blog,* http://theopedproject.word-
    press.com/.

8   Michael Wolff, "Politico's Washington Coup,"
    Vanity Fair, August 2009.

9   Tracy Mayor, "Soccer Mom Loses Her Kick,"
    Brain, Child Magazine, Fall 2007.

10 "Wal-Mart Moms Up for Grabs This
    November," Wal-Mart Stores, Inc., http://www.
    walmartcommunity.com/walmart-moms.

11 Ron Elving, "Weary Working Women
    May Be the Key to Midterms," *NPR.com,*
    September 28, 2010, http://www.npr.org/
    blogs/itsallpolitics/2010/09/28/130186841/-
    weary-working-women-may-be-the-key-to-2010-
    election-results.

12 Tracy Mayor, "Soccer Mom Loses Her Kick,"
    Brain, Child Magazine, Fall 2007.

13 Women's Media Center video, http://www.
    youtube.com/watch?v=QCfBAAOPZ98; The
    Op-Ed Project, http://www.theopedproject.org.

14 "Election 2010: Scorecard for Women
    Candidates," Center for American Women and
    Politics, Rutgers University website, http://
    www.cawp.rutgers.edu/fast_facts/elections/
    candidates_2010.php.

15 Lisa Witter, Lisa Chen, *The She Spot: Why
    Women Are the Market for Changing the
    World—And How to Reach Them* (Berrett-
    Koehler Publishers 2008).

16 "In the World of Social Media, Women Rule,"
    Brian Solis blog, October 3, 2009 http://www.
    briansolis.com/2009/10/in-world-of-social-
    media-women-rule.

17 "Mothers Know Best," *Fox & Friends, Fox
    News,* May 17, 2010, http://video.foxnews.
    com/v/4199981/mother-knows-best.

18 BlogHer/Compass Partners Survey, "2009
    Women and Social Media Study," http://www.
    blogher.com/2009-women-and-social-media-
    study.

19 Auren Hoffman, "The Social Media Gender
    Gap," *Bloomberg Business Week Online,* May
    19, 2008, http://www.businessweek.com/tech-
    nology/content/may2008/tc20080516_580743.
    htm.

20 Marisa Taylor, "Women Outnumber Men on
    Social Networking Sites," *Wall Street Journal
    Online,* October 7, 2009, http://blogs.wsj.com/
    digits/2009/10/07/women-outnumber-men-on-
    social-networking-sites.

21 "Influence is Bliss: The Gender Divide of
    Influence on Twitter," *Brian Solis blog,* August
    4, 2010, http://www.briansolis.com/2010/08/in-
    fluence-is-bliss-the-gender-divide-of-influence-
    on-twitter.

22 Noreen Malone, "Can Mama Grizzlies Pull Off
    a Twitter Revolution?" *Slate.com,* October 14,
    2010, http://www.slate.com/id/2270483.

23 Grace J. Yoo, Emily H. Zimmerman, and
    Katherine Preston, "The Obama Effect:
    Multidisciplinary Renderings of the 2008
    Campaign," in *Mothers Out to Change U.S.
    Politics: Obama Mamas Involved and Engaged,*
    ed. Heather Harris, Kimberly Moffitt,
    Catherine Squires, (State University of New
    York Press, 2010).

24 Jessica Faye Carter, "For Women, Social Media
    is More Than Girl Talk," *Mashable.com,* July
    17, 2010, http://mashable.com/2010/07/17/
    women-social-media.

25 Elisa Camahort Page, "BlogHer Goes to
    Washington," *Slideshare.net,* 2009, http://
    www.slideshare.net/ElisaCamahortPage/
    blogher-goes-to-washington.

26 Lisa Miller, "Hear Them Growl," *Newsweek,*
    September 27, 2010.

27 Michael Joseph Gross, "Sarah Palin: The Sound and The Fury," *Vanity Fair*, October, 2010; Diane Clehane, "Can Michelle Obama End the Mommy Wars," *vanityfair.com*, November 19 2008, http://www.vanityfair.com/online/daily/2008/11/can-michelle-obama-end-the-mommy-wars.html; Leslie Bennetts, "First Lady in Waiting," *vanityfair.com*, December 27, 2007, http://www.vanityfair.com/politics/features/2007/12/michelle_obama200712; Sandra Sobieraj Westfall, "John McCain and Sarah Palin: Shattering The Glass Ceiling," *people.com*, August 29, 2008, http://www.people.com/people/article/0,,20222685,00.html; "First Daughters White House Rules," *people.com*, February 25, 2009, http://www.people.com/people/article/0,,20261292,00.html.

28 Rebecca Johnson, "Sarah Palin: Altered State," *Vogue*, February 2008.

29 Francesca Donner, "Can Motherhood and Politics Mix?," *Wall Street Journal Front Lines blog*, September 8, 2008, http://blogs.wsj.com/frontlines/2008/09/08/can-politics-and-motherhood-mix/.

30 Kara Jesella, "Are Motherhood Politics a Good Idea," *The American Prospect Online*, September 16, 2008, http://www.prospect.org/cs/articles?article=are_motherhood_politics_a_good_idea.

31 Jodi Kantor, Kate Zernicke & Catrin Einhorn, "Fusing Motherhood and Politics in a New Way, *New York Times*, September 7, 2008, A1.

32 Dana Goldstein, "The Mommy Mantra: Why Female Politicians Lose When They Brand Themselves as Mothers," *The American Prospect Online*, January 19, 2007, http://www.prospect.org/cs/articles?articleId=12391.

33 Sheryl Gay Stolberg, "Michelle Obama Hits Campaign Trail with Soft-Sell Message," *New York Times*, October 13, 2010, A24.

34 Sheryl Gay Stolberg, "First Lady Hits the Campaign Trail," *New York Times, The Caucus blog*, October 13, 2010, http://thecaucus.blogs.nytimes.com/2010/10/13/first-lady-hits-campaign-trail; Z. Byron Wolf, "Mom-in-Chief" Hits the Campaign Trail: Amid Year of GOP 'Mama Grizzlies,' Michelle Obama Plays Up Role as Mother," *ABCNews.go.com*, October 13, 2010, http://abcnews.go.com/Politics/vote-2010-elections-mom-chief-michelle-obama-hits/story?id=11870916.

35 Mama Grizzlies ad from *SarahPAC.com*, http://www.youtube.com/watch?v=fsUVL6ciK-c.

36 Jean Spencer, "Palin: 'Look Out for Stampede of Pink Elephants,'" *wsj.com, Washington Wire blog*, May 14, 2010, http://blogs.wsj.com/washwire/2010/05/14/palin-look-out-for-stampede-of-pink-elephants.

37 "Sarah Doesn't Speak for Me" ad from EMILY's List, http://www.youtube.com/watch?v=Womp99eEaic.

38 Carrie Langer & Jill Greenlee, "The Effects of Politicized Motherhood and Gender Identities on Political Attitudes and Perceptions of Political Candidates," presented at International Society of Political Psychology 32nd Annual Scientific Meeting, July 14, 2009, Dublin, Ireland.

39 Participant in conference call with Senator Amy Klobuchar, September 21, 2009, http://www.blogher.com/transcript-klobuchar-call; "Senator Klobuchar Discusses Health Care Reform with Other Senators," *Senator Amy Klobuchar website*, November 3, 2009, http://klobuchar.senate.gov/multimediagallery_detail.cfm?id=320436&.

40 Senator Kirsten Gillibrand, e-mail exchange with author, April 27, 2010; Jonathan Van Meter, "In Hillary's Footsteps: Kirsten Gillibrand," *Vogue*, November 2010.

41 Kim Gandy, interview on October 21, 2009.

42 Krystal Ball, interview on January 23, 2010.

43 Amy Sewell, interview on March 4, 2009.

44 Victoria Rierdan Hurley, interview on March 4, 2009.

45 Judith Stadtman Tucker, interview February 22, 2010; Judith Stadtman Tucker, "Motherhood Made Me Do It! or How I Became an Activist," *Mothers Movement Online website*, September 2005, http://www.mothersmovement.org/features/mhoodpapers/activist_mother/made_me_do_it.htm.

46 Mothers Movement Online website, http://www.mothersmovement.org/.

47 "The Power of Social Networking for Women," *BlogHer website*, http://www.slideshare.net/mgrindeland/the-power-of-social-networking-for-women-08-01-09-1804210.

48 "In the World of Social Media, Women Rule," *Brian Solis blog*, October 3, 2009, http://www.briansolis.com/2009/10/in-world-of-social-media-women-rule/.

49 "The Power of Social Networking for Women," *BlogHer website*, http://www.slideshare.net/mgrindeland/the-power-of-social-networking-for-women-08-01-09-1804210.

50 Kristin Rowe-Finkbeiner, interview on December 2, 2009. "Fast Facts: Mothers in the United States," *National Organization for Women website*, http://www.now.org/issues/mothers/facts.html.

51 Celinda Lake, Kellyanne Conway, Catherine Whitney, *What Women Really Want: How American Women Are Quietly Erasing Political, Racial, Class and Religious Lines to Change the Way We Live*, (Free Press, 2005).

52 Kristin Rowe-Finkbeiner, interview on December 2, 2009; Lynn Harris, "Mom.com: The Virtual Power of Moms," *Parents Magazine,* February 2010.

53 Grace Yoo, "Motherhood and Politics: The Barack Obama Presidential Campaign," presented at American Sociological Association Annual Meeting, August 8, 2009, San Francisco, California.

54 *Blue Star Families website,* http://www.blue-starfam.org/resources/Surveys.

55 Update on Bisphenol A for Use in Food Contact Applications, *Food and Drug Administration website,* January 2010, http://www.fda.gov/NewsEvents/PublicHealthFocus/ucm197739.htm; "FDA Issues Warning About BPA Exposure," *CBSNews.com,* January 18, 2010, http://www.cbsnews.com/stories/2010/01/18/earlyshow/health/main6110716.shtml.

56 Kristen Chase, e-mail exchange with author, October 30, 2009.

57 Teri Christoph, e-mail exchange with author, May 16, 2010.

58 Glennia Campbell, e-mail exchange with author, December 8, 2009; "About the MOMocrats, *MOMocrats website,* http://momocrats.typepad.com/momocrats/about-momocratscom.html.

59 I am one of the original contributors to the MOMocrats blog.

60 Katherine Seeyle, "Women, Politics and the Internet, Part II," *New York Times Online,* October 15, 2007, http://www.nytimes.com/2007/10/15/us/politics/15web-seelye.html?_r=2&8dpc&oref=slogin.

61 Joan Blades, interview on December 14, 2009. MomsRising in 2010 also produced a similar video for the "Mother of the Decade."

62 Dee Dee Myers, interview on January 5, 2010.

63 Sarah Palin, *Going Rogue: An American Life,* (HarperCollins, 2009), Andrew Sullivan, "Going Rogue: The Fact Check Continues," *The Atlantic, The Daily Dish blog,* December 3, 2009, http://andrewsullivan.theatlantic.com/the_daily_dish/2009/12/the-odd-lies-of-sarah-palin-xxxvii-the-2006-abortion-debate.html.

64 Cyberhood is Powerful, Ms. Magazine, Summer 2009, http://www.msmagazine.com/summer2009/mommyblogs.asp

65 Blogger conference call with CNN producers, January 13, 2010.

66 Eric Kohn, "Discuss: Do Politics Belong in Kids' Movies?," *Moviefone.com,* http://blog.moviefone.com/2008/06/28/discuss-do-politics-belong-in-kids-movies/.

67 "Campaign '08 Not Just for Adults – Kids Love It," *MSNBC.com,* February 8, 2008, http://www.msnbc.msn.com/id/23075944/; Ron Dicker, "Parents are Party-Training Kids," *CNN.com,* February 4, 2008, http://www.cnn.com/2008/LIVING/wayoflife/02/04/politykes/index.html; Julie Just, "Politics and Kids," *New York Times, Paper Cuts blog,* October 10, 2008, http://papercuts.blogs.nytimes.com/2008/10/10/politics-and-kids/; PBS Democracy Project, http://pbskids.org/democracy.

68 Nia Malika-Henderson, "Right Blasts Obama Speech to Students," *Politico.com,* September 3, 2009, http://www.politico.com/news/stories/0909/26711.html; "Republican Party of Florida says Obama will "indoctrinate" school children with "socialist ideology," *Politifact website,* September 2, 2009, http://politifact.com/truth-o-meter/statements/2009/sep/02/republican-party-florida/republican-party-florida-says-obama-will-indoctrin.

69 "Pep Talk or Indoctrination?," CNN.com, *Blogger Bunch,* September 8, 2009, http://www.cnn.com/video/#/video/politics/2009/09/08/dcl.blog.obama.speech.cnn; Lou Dobbs Calls Obama's Back to School Speech and Children Singing "Indoctrination in the Classroom," *Crooks and Liars blog,* October 1, 2009, http://videocafe.crooksandliars.com/heather/lou-dobbs-calls-obamas-back-school-speech; Statement issued by Florida Republican Party Chairman Jim Greer, http://www.rpof.org/article.php?id=754.

70 James C. McKinley & Sam Dillon, "Some Parents Oppose Obama School Speech," *New York Times,* September 4, 2009, A1; Joshua Rhett Miller, "Critics Decry Obama's 'Indoctrination' Plan for Students," *FoxNews.com,* September 2, 2009, http://www.foxnews.com/politics/2009/09/02/critics-decry-obamas-indoctrination-plan-students.

71 "Obama's September 8 speech to schoolchildren," *Michelle Malkin blog,* September 1, 2009, http://michellemalkin.com/2009/09/01/obamas-sept-8-speech-to-schoolchildren/

72 Michael Alison Chandler & Michael D. Shear, "Backlash Growing Over Obama School Speech," *CBSNews,com,* September 4, 2009, http://www.cbsnews.com/stories/2009/09/04/politics/washingtonpost/main5288013.shtml ; "Obama School Speech: Lesson or Propaganda?," *wsj.com, Washington Wire blog,* September 3, 2009, http://blogs.wsj.com/washwire/2009/09/03/obama-school-speech-lesson-or-propaganda/; "Beck calls Obama's stay –in-school speech to students "indoctrination," *Media Matters website,* September 2, 2009, http://mediamatters.org/mmtv/200909020011.

73 "Laura Bush defends Obama School Speech," *CNN.com, Political Ticker blog,* September 7, 2009, http://politicalticker.blogs.cnn.com/2009/09/07/laura-bush-defends-obama-school-speech/.

74 Joshua Rhett Miller, "Critics Decry Obama's 'Indoctrination' Plan for Students," *Foxnews.com,* September 2, 2009, http://www.foxnews.com/politics/2009/09/02/critics-decry-obamas-indoctrination-plan-students/; Nia Malika-Henderson, "Right blasts Obama speech to children," *Politico.com,* September 3, 2009, http://www.politico.com/news/stories/0909/26711.html.

75 Anne Duncan, "Barack Obama is not the first president to address schoolchildren," *Politifact.com,* August 26, 2009, http://www.politifact.com/truth-o-meter/statements/2009/sep/03/arne-duncan/barack-obama-not-first-president-address-school-ch/; Text of George H.W. Bush speech to schoolchildren, 1991, http://bushlibrary.tamu.edu/research/public_papers.php?id=3450&year=1991&month=10; Ronald Reagan speech broadcast via radio and TV to schoolchildren, http://www.reagan.utexas.edu/archives/speeches/1986/51386d.htm.

76 "An interview with Katharine DeBrecht," *Intellectual Conservative blog,* http://www.intellectualconservative.com/article4625.html.

77 Hollie McKay, "Sarah Palin Stars as Heroine in New Children's Book," *Foxnews.com,* December 1, 2009, http://www.foxnews.com/entertainment/2009/12/01/sarah-palin-stars-heroine-new-childrens-books/?test=faces; Kate Henka, "Author's Corner: Katharine DeBrecht," *CapitolWeekly.net,* December 16, 2009, http://www.capitolweekly.net/article.php?xid=yhngg55jhopssk.

78 Catherine Rampbell, "Raising a Political Bigot," *WashingtonPost.com,* August 11, 2007,, http://www.washingtonpost.com/wp-dyn/content/article/2007/08/10/AR2007081001691.html.

79 Melinda Henneberger, interview on January 2, 2010.

80 Michael McDevitt, "The Partisan Child: Developmental Provocation as a Model of Political Socialization," *International Journal of Public Opinion Research,* 18(1) (April 1, 2005): 67-88.

81 Oxygen/Markle Pulse Survey, "American Mothers are Primary Influence on Women's Political Behavior and Attitudes," June 13, 2000, http://www.markle.org/news/press_releases/2000/press_release_06132000.php.

82 Grace J. Yoo, Emily H. Zimmerman, and Katherine Preston, "The Obama Effect: Multidisciplinary Renderings of the 2008 Campaign," in *Mothers Out to Change U.S. Politics: Obama Mamas Involved and Engaged,* ed. Heather Harris, Kimberly Moffitt, Catherine Squires, (State University of New York Press, 2010).

83 Dee Dee Myers, interview on January 5, 2010; Dee Dee Myers, e-mail exchange with author, February 16, 2010.

84 The Dreyfuss Initiative, http://www.thedreyfussinitiative.org/what-we-do/the-initiative.html; Richard Dreyfuss, "Civics Unrest: On Teaching Our Kids to Love Democracy," *Edutopia blog,* http://www.edutopia.org/civics-unrest-teaching-kids-to-love-democracy; Richard Dreyfuss, "We Must Resume Teaching Civics, *San Diego Union online,* September 17, 2009, "http://www.signonsandiego.com/news/2009/sep/17/we-must-resume-teaching-civics.

85 Lilly Ledbetter sued her longtime employer, Goodyear Tire and Rubber Co., for wage and gender discrimination, presenting evidence that men in the same position that she held were paid higher salaries than she was. Ledbetter ultimately lost her case when the Supreme Court ruled in 2007, she was barred from recovering the money because she had waited too long to file her claim. In 2009, the first bill signed into law by President Barack Obama was the Lilly Ledbetter Fair Pay Act, reversing the Supreme Court, expanding the time within which any employee is permitted to seek back pay for wage discrimination. http://edlabor.house.gov/lilly-ledbetter-fair-pay-act/index.shtml.

86 The Mother PAC, http://www.motherpac.org/; The Kitchen Cabinet PAC, http://www.thekitchencabinetpac.com/; SarahPAC, http://www.sarahpac.com.

87 Celinda Lake, Kellyanne Conway, Catherine Whitney, *What Women Really Want, How American Women Are Quietly Erasing Political, Racial, Class, and Religious Lines to Change the Way We Live,* (Free Press, 2005).

88 Kathryn Jean Lopez, "Politics from the Kitchen Table," *National Review Online,* October 5, 2010, http://www.nationalreview.com/corner/248830/politics-kitchen-table-kathryn-jean-lopez#.

89 Grace J. Yoo, Emily H. Zimmerman, and Katherine Preston, "The Obama Effect: Multidisciplinary Renderings of the 2008 Campaign," in *Mothers Out to Change U.S. Politics: Obama Mamas Involved and Engaged,* ed. Heather Harris, Kimberly Moffitt, Catherine Squires, (State University of New York Press, 2010); Jill S. Greenlee, "Soccer Moms, Hockey Moms, and the Question of Transformative Motherhood," *Politics & Gender,* 2010.

90 Brad Knickerbocker, "Democrats rally behind their 'mom in tennis shoes,' Sen. Patty Murray," *Christian Science Monitor online,* September 29, 2010, http://www.csmonitor.com/USA/Election-2010/Senate/2010/0929/Democrats-rally-behind-their-mom-in-tennis-shoes-Sen.-Patty-Murray.

91 Gail Sheehy, "Hillaryland at War," *Vanity Fair,* September 2008.

92 "Most Voters Say Children Motivate Mothers in Political Office," *Rasmussen Reports,* October, 2008, http://www.rasmussenreports.com/public_content/politics/elections/election_2008/2008_presidential_election/most_voters_say_children_motivate_mothers_in_political_office.

93 Emily Bazelon, "Palin the Ever Lovin' Mother," *Slate.com,* November 16, 2009, http://www.doublex.com/blog/xxfactor/palin-ever-lovin-mother.

94 Mama Grizzlies ad, SarahPAC, http://www.youtube.com/watch?v=fsUVL6ciK-c.

95 Leslie Sanchez, *You've Come a Long Way, Maybe: Sarah, Michelle, Hillary and the Shaping of the New American Woman,* (Palgrave Macmillan, 2009).

96 Leslie Sanchez, interview on January 14, 2010.

97 Susan J. Carroll, *"Security Moms and Presidential Politics",* in *Voting the Gender Gap,* ed. Lois Duke Whitaker, (University of Illinois Press, 2009).

98 Melinda Henneberger, *If They Only Listened to Us: What Women Voters Want Politicians to Hear* (Simon & Schuster, 2007).

99 Melinda Henneberger, interview on January 2, 2010.

100 Emily McKhann and Cooper Munroe, interview on November 4, 2009.

101 Joan Blades, interview on December 14, 2009.

102 Kristin Rowe-Finkbeiner, interview on December 2, 2009; Claudia Rowe, "Kristin Rowe-Finkbeiner mobilizes moms to fight for their rights," *The Seattle Times online,* December 13, 2009.

103 Claudia Rowe, "Midterm Elections: Families Will Determine the Outcome," *The Seattle Times, Seattle City Brights blog,* November 1, 2010, Claudia Rowe, "Midterm Elections: Families Will Determine the Outcome," *The Seattle Times, Seattle City Brights blog,* November 1, 2010.

104 CBS News/New York Times Poll, "Hillary Clinton, Women Voters and the 2008 Election," *Center for American Women and Politics, Rutgers University website,* July 9-17, 2007, http://www.cawp.rutgers.edu/fast_facts/elections/documents/08-CBSNYT_HClinton_gendergap.pdf; Katharine Q. Seelye, *"In Poll, Women Are Supportive But Skeptical of Clinton,"* New York Times website, July 19, 2007, http://www.nytimes.com/2007/07/19/us/politics/19cnd-poll.html.

105 Jack Cafferty, "Best debate strategy for Clinton?," *CNN.com, Cafferty File blog,* February 26, 2008, http://caffertyfile.blogs.cnn.com/2008/02/26/best-debate-strategy-for-clinton.

106 Liz Hunt, "How good a 'mom' can Sarah Palin be," *The Telegraph online,* September 3, 2008, http://www.telegraph.co.uk/comment/columnists/lizhunt/3561880/How-good-a-mom-can-Sarah-Palin-be.html.

107 Lyndsey Layton, "Moms in the House, With Kids at Home," *Washington Post online,* July 19, 2007, http://www.washingtonpost.com/wp-dyn/content/article/2007/07/18/AR2007071802167.html.

108 Jodi Kantor & Rachel L. Swarns, "A New Twist in the Debate on Mothers," *New York Times,* September 1, 2008, A1.

109 Stephanie Mencimer, "Will Sarah Palin Bring a Breast Pump on the Campaign Trail?," *Mother Jones, Mojo blog,* August 29, 2008, http://motherjones.com/print/8595.

110 Jura Koncias, "The gentlemom from New York: Sen. Kirsten Gillibrand's work-life balance", *Washington Post online,* December 17, 2009, http://www.washingtonpost.com/wp-dyn/content/article/2009/12/15/AR2009121503978.html.

111 "CNN's Beck mimed Hillary Clinton shaving her face," *Media Matters for America website,* December 18, 2007, http://mediamatters.org/research/200712180007.

112 John F. Harris & Beth Frerking, "Clinton aides: Palin treatment sexist," *Politico.com,* September 3, 2008, http://www.politico.com/news/stories/0908/13129.html.

113 Reid Pillifant "Senator Working Mom Beefing with Meat Industry," *The New York Observer online, Politicker NY blog,* June 4, 2010, http://www.observer.com/2010/politics/senator-working-mom-beefing-meat-industry; Brian Tumulty, "'Senator Mom' Kirsten Gillibrand faces 'I told you so' Joe DioGuardi in U.S. Senate race," *stargaazette.com,* October 19, 2010, http://www.stargazette.com/article/20101019/NEWS01/10190359/-Senator-Mom-faces-I-told-you-so-Joe-in-U-S-Senate-race.

114 U.S. Senator Kirsten Gillibrand, e-mail exchange with author, April 27, 2010.

115 Julie Sullivan, *"For Women, Work and Family Create Political Minefield," The Oregonian online,* September 6, 2008, http://www.oregonlive.com/news/index.ssf/2008/09/for_women_work_and_family_crea.html.

116 Shelley Correll, interview on February 2, 2010.

117 *Debbie Wasserman Schultz on Carrying a Crayon video,* March 10, 2010, Get a Women Elected event, Arlington, Virginia, http://www.youtube.com/watch?v=eatRLG3PXME.

118 Jill Miller Zimon, *"Tackling the Number One Reason Women Don't Run for Office," BlogHer website,* August 2, 2010, http://www.blogher.com/no-excuses-allowed-tackling-1-reason-women-dont-run-office.

119 Aimee Olivo, e-mail exchange with author, November 17, 2010.

120 Julie Sullivan, *"For Women, Work and Family Create Political Minefield," The Oregonian online,* September 6, 2008, http://www.oregonlive.com/news/index.ssf/2008/09/for_women_work_and_family_crea.html/.

121 http://en.wikipedia.org/wiki/Dooce.

122 Leslie Sanchez, interview on January 14, 2010.

123 Dee Dee Myers, telephone interview on January 5, 2010; Dee Dee Myers, e-mail exchange with author, February 16, 2010.

124 Tarryl Clark, interview on December 14, 2009.

125 Robin Roberts, "Political Mommy Wars, Who is the Best Leader?,"*ABCnews.go.com,* October 26, 2010, http://abcnews.go.com/GMA/Parenting/video/marriage-children-mom-qualified-governor-11971032.

126 Jennifer Lawless & Richard Fox, "Why Are Women Still Not Running for Office," *Brown Policy Report,* Brown University, March 2008.

127 Jill Miller Zimon, "No Excuses Allowed: Tackling the Number One Reason Women Don't Run for Office," *BlogHer website,* August 2, 2010, http://www.blogher.com/no-excuses-allowed-tackling-1-reason-women-dont-run-office; Jennifer Lawless & Richard Fox, "Why Are Women Still Not Running for Office," *Brown Policy Report,* Brown University, March 2008; Jennifer Lawless, interview February 2010; Jennifer Lawless & Richard Fox, *It Still Takes a Candidate: Why Women Don't Run for Office* (Cambridge University Press, 2010).

128 Siobhan "Sam" Bennett, interview on December 14, 2009.

129 Siobhan "Sam" Bennett, interview on December 14, 2009.

130 Corina Fiore, e-mail exchange with author, April 21, 2010.

131 The Conversation Blog, RNC Day 3: Sarah Palin, Working Mother, http://blogs.hbr.org/cs/2008/09/rnc_day_3_sarah_palin_and_fami.html.

132 The G-Spot blog, http://www.thegspot.typepad.com/.

133 Michael Calderone, "New Pundits: Prodigies or Pipsqueaks?," *Politico.com,* April 9, 2010, http://www.politico.com/news/stories/0410/35564.html.

134 Robin Marty, "Where are the Women Pundits?" *Care2.com website,* April 21, 2010, http://www.care2.com/causes/womens-rights/blog/where-are-the-women-pundits.

135 Sara Libby, "What About the Next Great Female Pundit?," *Salon.com, Broadsheet blog,* April 12, 2010, http://www.salon.com/life/broadsheet/2010/04/12/americas_next_great_male_pundit.

136 *The Byline Blog,* http://theopedproject.wordpress.com.

137 Shelley J. Correll, interview on February 2, 2010.

138 Marian Wang, "Where are All the Lady Bloggers," *Mother Jones online, The Riff blog,* October 29, 2009, http://motherjones.com/riff/2009/10/where-are-all-lady-bloggers.

139 National Public Radio Ombudsman report by Alicia Shepard, "Where are the Women?," *NPR.com,* April 2, 2010, http://www.npr.org/blogs/ombudsman/2010/04/where_are_the_women.html.

140 "Marketing to Women Report," *She-conomy blog,* http://she-conomy.com/report/facts-on-women/; *Washington Post* online chat with pollsters Celinda Lake and Kellyanne Conway, October 27, 2005, http://www.washingtonpost.com/wp-dyn/content/discussion/2005/10/25/DI2005102500919.html.